EGBE ORUN

The Soul Group That Remembers You

ALSO BY DR. LA TOYA DAVIS

- *Accessing the Akashic Records: A Practical Guide to Healing, Clarity, and Empowerment*

- *The Akashic Record Journal: A Guided Journal to Support Accessing and Exploring Your Akashic Records*

- *Path to the Ancestors: 33 Prayers, Prompts, and Rituals for Healing and Connection*

- *Path to the Ancestors: 33 Day Guided Journal for Healing, Connection, and Personal Growth*

- *Odu Ifá: A Coloring & Activity Book to Learn the 16 Major Odu*

- *Gratitude Journal: 6 Week Journey to Creating an Attitude of Gratitude*

To View Books, Scan the QR Code:

EGBE ORUN

The Soul Group That Remembers You

~

Understanding Your Pre-Birth Agreements Through Yoruba Cosmology and Universal Consciousness

Dr. La Toya Davis

Ìyá Ẹgbẹ́níkẹ́

Published by CHI Publishing

ISBN Paperback: 978-1-959406-22-8
ISBN EBook: 978-1-959406-22-8

Library of Congress Control Number: 2026900798

First Edition

www.chipublishing.com

DEDICATION

"We are always and forever the summation of all of our parts."
Dr. La Toya Davis

This book is dedicated to all of the "parts" that have landed me
where I am today.
To the good, the bad, and the in-between…I give thanks.

To all the members of my various Egbe Aiye, I'm glad we get to live
this life together.

Call: Ẹgbẹ́ o!

Response: Àkíkà! Àsègé! Ojú ò ní wà t'ọ̀.

—

Àkíkà! — Strength, steadfastness, resilience.

Àsègé! — Victory, success, uplift, triumph.

Ojú ò ní wà t'ọ̀. — You will not be put to shame. You will not be disgraced. You will not be ridiculed.

Traditional greeting between Ẹgbẹ́ devotees and priests

Ẹsẹ̀ Ifá (Yorùbá)

Òwúkè, wúkè

Tí jẹ omọ bí ìtalẹ̀

Ẹgbẹ́ omakoko, Ó gìyàn Àbíkú

Oníyànjú owó, Àdìndìn Odí

Ẹgbẹ́ Ọ̀run Gba mi

Kí Ẹgbẹ́ Ayé má tẹ́.

~

English Translation

The society of Heaven and Earth

Those who tunnel the soil together

And eat people like termites

The children of the herbs

The group who differentiates life from death

And make profit from business

Egbe of Heaven have mercy on me

So that the Egbe of life will not laugh.

From Odù Ifá Odi Meji

CONTENTS

Author's Note

Before you begin, I want you to know what this book is and what it isn't.

This is not an academic text on Yoruba religion. It is not a manual for traditional Egbe practice. It is not an instruction guide for conducting ceremonies or initiations. If you're looking for any of those things, I'll point you toward the scholars and practitioners (in the Appendix) whose work has made this book possible, and whose expertise in traditional practice far exceeds mine.

What this book offers is a bridge.

I am an initiated Egbe priestess, but I am also a child of the African diaspora. I came up through Lucumí. I've been initiated in Palo Mayombe. I practice Isese. I am also an Akashic Records practitioner who has read for thousands of clients and trained hundreds of students. I live at the intersection of traditional African spirituality and universal metaphysics, and I've spent years trying to understand how these systems illuminate each other.

This book shares what I've discovered: that Egbe Orun, the Yoruba concept of heavenly soul groups, describes something universal about how consciousness works. That the soul agreements you made before birth are real, accessible, and actively shaping your life. That you don't need initiation to understand yourself as part of a spiritual collective that remembers who you are when you forget.

I write from within the Yoruba tradition because that's where this framework originates and where it has remained most intact. But I also write for seekers from all paths who sense that there's something larger orchestrating their lives, something they can't quite name but recognize.

If that's you, this book is for you.

You don't have to convert to anything. You don't have to abandon your existing spiritual framework. You just have to be willing to consider that the soul group dynamics described in these pages have been guiding your life all along, whether you knew the Yoruba words for them or not.

One more thing: Throughout this book, I share personal stories from my own journey and from client sessions. Where client stories appear, details have been changed to protect privacy, but the spiritual patterns are real. I've received permission to share what I share, and I've honored the request for anonymity where it was given.

Now. Let's begin.

Dr. La Toya Davis
Ìyá Ẹgbẹ́níkẹ́

How to Use This Book

This book bridges two worlds: Yoruba cosmology and universal metaphysics. Whether you're coming to this work as someone familiar with African Traditional Religions or as a spiritual seeker discovering Egbe for the first time, you'll encounter terminology from both frameworks.

If you're new to Yoruba concepts: You'll find words like Egbe, Ori, Enikeji Orun, Aiye, and Orun throughout. Don't worry about memorizing them all at once. A comprehensive Glossary of Terms is available at the back of this book for easy reference. I recommend bookmarking it.

If you're new to metaphysical concepts: Terms like Akashic Records, Law of Correspondence, soul contracts, and universal consciousness are woven throughout. These are also defined in the Glossary.

How to read this book: You can read straight through from beginning to end, or you can start with whatever chapter title calls to you. The concepts build on each other, but each chapter is also designed to stand on its own.

The Appendices at the back contain: practical prayers and invocations you can use immediately, a list of traditional offerings to Egbe, and journaling prompts to deepen your work.

This is not an academic text. This is wisdom passed through lived experience, initiation, and years of spiritual practice. Take what resonates. Leave what doesn't. Trust your own knowing as you read.

The book is organized in four parts.

Part I: Foundations introduces you to Egbe, your Enikeji Orun (eternal soul self), and the Universal Field where all consciousness exists. This section establishes the cosmological framework we'll build on throughout.

Part II: Correspondence goes deep into the Law of Correspondence and how it explains the mechanics of soul agreements. You'll learn about the choices your Ori made before birth and how your Egbe orchestrates circumstances to fulfill them.

Part III: Alignment and Integration focuses on practical application. How do you recognize when you're in alignment with your soul agreements? How do you work with resistance? How do you distinguish between Egbe, ancestors, guides, and other spiritual forces?

Part IV: Expansion widens the frame to consider what happens across lifetimes, how to integrate all parts of yourself, and what it means to live as a bridge between Orun and Aiye.

Each chapter includes reflection questions to deepen your engagement with the material. The Appendices at the back provide prayers, offerings, and practical tools you can use immediately.

Read in order if you want the full conceptual build. Skip to whatever calls you if you prefer to follow your intuition. Both approaches work.

PART I

FOUNDATIONS

Before we can work with our soul agreements, we have to understand what we're working with.

Part I establishes the cosmology. This is where you meet the core players in your spiritual ecosystem: Egbe Orun, the soul group that witnessed your pre-birth choices and continues to orchestrate your path. Enikeji Orun, your eternal soul self that carries your essence across lifetimes. And the Universal Field, the infinite consciousness where all of this exists and intersects.

These aren't abstract concepts. They're aspects of you, operating across dimensions, shaping your life whether you're aware of them or not.

In the next three chapters, you'll learn what Egbe actually is and why understanding it changes everything about how you navigate your life. You'll meet your Enikeji Orun and understand how it relates to your Ori and your Egbe. And you'll see how the Akashic Records, the Universal Field, and Yoruba cosmology all point to the same truth from different angles.

This is the foundation everything else builds on. Take your time here. Let the concepts settle. The practical work of Parts II, III, and IV will land differently once you truly understand what you're made of.

Let's begin.

CHAPTER 1

EGBE ORUN:
THE SOUL GROUP THAT
REMEMBERS YOU

PART 1: THE PERSONAL JOURNEY

I still remember the moment everything changed.

I was preparing for my Obatala initiation in 2015, about to take a major step in my spiritual journey, when my godfather suggested we do a Misa first. A Misa is a spiritual gathering where we invite the ancestors and spirits to come through and deliver messages. It's powerful work, and he wanted clarity before we moved forward.

During that Misa, he sat there looking at me, listening. Then he shook his head.

"No," he said. "Something's off. I'm missing something."

He paused, tuning in deeper to whatever he was hearing from spirit, and then he looked directly at me.

"I don't think this is the right path for you. I think you're supposed to be initiated to Egbe."

Egbe.

I had never heard that word in my life.

What strikes me as significant is that I had been practicing African Traditional Religions for over a decade at that point. Lucumí (also known as Santería, the Cuban Orisa tradition) was my foundation. I knew the Orisa, understood the cosmology, worked ceremonies. I'd been initiated in Palo Mayombe. I'd devoted fifteen years to these spiritual practices.

But here was my godfather telling me about something called Egbe, and I'd never encountered it. Not once. Not in any ceremony, any conversation, any teaching I'd received in all those years.

What I Didn't Know Then

What struck me later (much later, after I'd done the work and started processing the experience of Nigeria) was the significance of that gap.

Through divination in Lucumí, I had repeatedly been told to work with Ibeji, the sacred twins. I did the offerings, followed the guidance, honored what came through. But honestly? It never fully resonated. Something in my spirit always said "this doesn't make sense," but I did what I was told.

Looking back, I think those early divinations were picking up on Egbe, but since Egbe wasn't a concept we worked with at that time in Lucumí, it got interpreted as the closest thing available, Ibeji. Both deal with spiritual companionship, both involve multiple souls, both deal with children. I can see how they'd read similarly in divination, especially if the full Egbe framework wasn't available.

This isn't anyone's fault. This is just how cultural preservation works under impossible circumstances. When Africans were forcibly enslaved and had to figure out how to maintain knowledge across the Middle Passage, things got conflated, absorbed, reinterpreted. What matters is that the essence survived, even if the specific framework didn't make it intact into every diasporic tradition.

Egbe, as a distinct theological concept with its own cosmology, largely didn't survive the Trans-Atlantic slave trade the way many Orisa did. In Yoruba Isese tradition, Egbe was never lost. It never stopped being understood, honored, and worked with as a deity. It has its own rituals, its own priesthood, its own place in the spiritual ecosystem.

But in the diaspora traditions I knew? At that time, it wasn't there.

One of my biggest "aha" moments upon returning from Nigeria was realizing that in the preservation attempts of our ancestors, Egbe was syncretized with Ibeji. How did I arrive at that? I noticed that many of the ways Ibeji was propitiated in the diaspora was actually how Egbe was propitiated and talked about in Nigeria. Meanwhile, Ibeji (the Lucumí/Isese correlation) was vastly different. But if I looked at the two together, it made sense.

So I Got on a Plane

My godfather didn't hesitate once he received the confirmation through divination. He said, "I know this is what you need," and he sent me to Nigeria to be initiated.

What I'm forever grateful for: he didn't let his ego get in the way. He could have said, "Well, I can still do the Obatala initiation because that's what I know how to do." But he didn't. He honored what spirit was telling him, even if it meant sending me somewhere else.

So I got on a plane. Didn't know exactly where I was going, didn't know who I'd be meeting, didn't fully understand what Egbe even was. But I trusted him, and I trusted the process.

He sent me to meet Fúnláyọ Wood in Nigeria. She was one of my godfather's students, conducting research on the use of kola nut. I'd met her before, so at least I'd have a familiar face when I landed. (She's the founder of Asé Ire Inc and doing incredible work bridging tradition and contemporary practice, but back then, she was just the person picking me up from the airport.)

The Research

Before I left, I tried to do my homework. There was exactly one book available at the time: *Egbe: The Heavenly Mates of Every Human* by Ayo Salami. The book has recently gone into reprint (2024) as the original printing is no longer available.

I read that book over and over because it was all I had. Now there are more resources. Ifayemisi Elebuibon has written beautifully on Egbe in her books *Egbe Orun: Comrades of Heaven* (2020) and *Egbe Orun Path to Self Discovery* (2023). There's another book called *Egbe: The Sacred Tie That Binds* by Baale Olukunmi Omikemi Egbelade (2016). But back then, it was just me and that one text, trying to understand what I was walking into.

The Initiation

I spent a few days in Ibadan with Fúnláyọ, getting acclimated to Nigeria. Then we journeyed to Osogbo, where I was received by Araba Chief Ifayemi Elebuibon and his wife Iyalorisa Oyelola Ajibola Elebuibon.

Their compound was the kind of place where you could feel the weight of lineage. Generations of knowledge held in every corner. They welcomed me, fed me, cared for me in ways that reminded me why I love this tradition. There's a level of genuine care that happens in African Traditional Religions when you visit someone's space that I deeply appreciate. It's like good Southern hospitality, but amplified.

I got initiated in July 2015, and it changed everything. Not in some vague, mystical way. In a very real, very tangible way. My godfather told me during that Misa, "You have too many spiritual gifts. If I initiate you to Obatala, I fear those gifts will be muted. And I think that would be a disservice to you."

He was right.

I'd always been intuitive. I'd always had the gift of sight (the ability to see things, know things, predict things), but I didn't really understand it. It was just something I'd lived with my whole life, this background hum of knowing that I couldn't always explain.

I had become well known in my spiritual community for my mediumship and my ability to "work" *the white table*, which means to lead or head a Misa. (The white table is central to Espiritismo and involves calling in spirits and ancestors to deliver messages.) My work as a spiritualist was draining and taxing on the body. I often had to go into possession to deliver messages.

After the Egbe initiation, that connection to spirit became amplified but also easier.

A few months after returning from Nigeria, I went to a Misa at my Palo Mayombe godsister's house in New York. Fresh off the "mat" (the initiation mat where ceremonies take place), still integrating everything that had happened. And for the first time in my life, I received successive messages without going into full possession. The information came through clearly. I went around to every single person in the room and provided a message with an ease I had never experienced before.

That's when I understood what had shifted. The initiation hadn't given me new gifts; it had heightened, or as I like to say 10x'd, the ones I already had.

But What I Received During Initiation

During the initiation ceremony, I received divination. This is standard practice. You're given guidance about your spiritual path and any taboos you need to observe. Taboos are specific things you should not do based on who you are spiritually and what your soul came here to accomplish. They can range from colors you can't wear, foods you can't eat, actions you can't participate in. It's not arbitrary, although it can seem that way. It's actually soul-level information, revealed through divination, about what your spirit cannot tolerate in this lifetime.

Mine was lying.

When I first heard this, I was genuinely confused. My first thought was: *I'm not a liar.*

Now, don't mistake that as me saying I never told a lie. But most people who know me would probably tell you I was honest to a fault. As a child, my mom said I wouldn't even lie about my age to get free admission and free food. I thought, Why would this be my taboo?

But months later, I'd understand they weren't talking about lying to others. They were pointing to the lies I was telling myself about my marriage, my career, my life. That taboo would become the thread that unraveled everything I'd been holding onto out of fear.

I realized I had been living a lie by conforming to societal expectations instead of following my soul's truth. I was maintaining a life that looked acceptable from the outside but felt hollow on the inside. I was doing things because that's what you're "supposed" to do (the career path, the relationship structure, the acceptable version of success) rather than listening to what my spirit was actually telling me it wanted.

I had learned to doubt my intuition, to silence my inner knowing, to prioritize other people's opinions over my own soul's voice. And that was the lie. That was the incongruence my Egbe was pointing to.

Once I saw it, I couldn't unsee it.

By June 2016, less than a year after the initiation, I had separated from my spouse and moved to Tallahassee to start a new position at Florida

State University. It was painful and simultaneously freeing. It required me to face judgments from others and from myself. But it was also the most honest thing I'd done in a long time.

And once I stopped lying to myself, once I started living according to my agreements instead of society's expectations, the doors started opening.

The Spread of Egbe Knowledge

When I came back from Nigeria in 2015, I looked for other Egbe practitioners here in the States. There just weren't many I could find. I was obsessed with learning everything I could. The knowledge existed, but it wasn't widely available or accessible.

But that's changed.

In the years since, I've watched Egbe knowledge make its way into other spiritual sectors. There are more initiated priests now, more people writing about it, more seekers discovering it through dreams, through downloads, through that familiar pull toward something they can't name but recognize.

The timing isn't coincidence. The energy of Egbe itself is pushing this knowing forward. It's like it's orchestrating its own revelation: nudging people to remember, sending downloads to those ready to receive, making its presence known in a way that feels both ancient and urgently contemporary.

Maybe this is part of what Egbe does: it recognizes when the collective consciousness is ready for certain information, and it activates the channels to get it through.

I have accepted that I am one of those channels. You might be another.

So let me tell you what Egbe actually is.

PART 2: WHAT EGBE ACTUALLY IS

A Note on Language: Yoruba vs. Isese

Before we go deeper, I want to clarify the language I'll be using throughout this book.

Yoruba refers to the people, the language, and the culture of the Yoruba ethnic group, primarily in Nigeria, Benin, and Togo.

Isese is the traditional religion and spiritual practice of the Yoruba people. The word means "tradition" or "origin" in the Yoruba language.

When I reference "Yoruba cosmology," I'm speaking about the worldview of the Yoruba people. When I reference "Isese practice" or "Isese teaching," I'm speaking specifically about the religious and spiritual framework.

I practice Isese. I was initiated in Osun State, Osogbo, Nigeria. The concepts of Egbe, Ori, and Enikeji Orun come from Isese theology. While I am writing from within that lineage, I also acknowledge that Orisa worship, and the cosmologies that accompany it, exist throughout the diaspora in forms such as Lucumí, Candomblé, Shango Baptist, Trinidad Orisa, and beyond. These traditions share common roots, even when their languages, rituals, and expressions have adapted over time.

We'll explore the universality of these concepts throughout this book, but for now, this grounding helps us begin from the same place.

A Note on Lineage and the Diaspora

I want to be transparent about something important: while my initiation and lineage are Isese, I am a child of the diaspora. That means the way I understand, practice, and teach this work has been shaped not only by mainland Yoruba tradition, but also by the retentions, adaptations, and evolutions that happened throughout the African diaspora.

I came up through Lucumí. I've been initiated in Palo Mayombe. I've studied Espiritismo. These traditions are part of my spiritual DNA, and they inform how I synthesize and communicate what I've learned.

When I reference concepts like spirit guides, for example, that language doesn't come directly from Isese cosmology. Spirit guides are a diasporic adaptation that emerged through practices like Espiritismo in Cuba and has since become part of how many of us in the Americas understand and work with spiritual forces.

I'm not trying to practice "straight Isese" the way it's practiced in Osogbo, and I'm not asking you to either. Most of us don't have daily access to elders in Nigeria. Most of us are working with what survived the Middle Passage, what got preserved under impossible circumstances, and what has continued to evolve as these traditions take root in new soil.

This book honors all of that. I teach Egbe through the lens of Yoruba cosmology because that's where the framework originates and where it has remained most intact. But I also teach it through the lens of universal metaphysics, Akashic Records, and consciousness principles because that's how I've come to understand it, and that's the bridge that makes this work accessible to seekers from all paths.

If you're coming to this work with your own spiritual background (whether that's Christianity, Buddhism, New Thought metaphysics, or no formal tradition at all), there's room for you here. Egbe isn't asking you to convert. It's asking you to recognize the soul group dynamics that have been guiding your life all along.

Starting From the Same Place

Meanings and definitions are shaped by our worldview. Two people can say the exact same word and still be talking about two entirely different things because the lens they're speaking from isn't the same. This happens all the time in spiritual spaces, especially in the diaspora, where the same terminology gets carried through different countries, languages, lineages, and lived experiences.

So before we build anything else, I want to make sure we're starting from the same place.

What I'm about to share isn't the singular definition of Egbe; it's the framework I'm using throughout this book, rooted in Isese theology, shaped by my initiation, and informed by what I've learned through direct experience. If you're brand new to this concept, this will give you a clear baseline. If you've heard of Egbe before, consider this your reference point for how I'm speaking about it.

From here on, when I say "Egbe" or "Egbe Orun," this is what I mean.

The Basic Definition

Let's start with the basics. In Yoruba, the word *Egbe* literally translates to "group" or "society." Not "spirit" or "deity" or "force." Group. It's a direct linguistic acknowledgment that you belong to a spiritual collective.

Egbe Orun means "heavenly society" or "heavenly group." It's the spiritual collective you belonged to before you were born, the one you belong to now, and the one you'll return to after this life. These are your heavenly mates, not romantic partners, but spiritual companions who share your soul's evolutionary journey.

In Yoruba cosmology, before you came to Aiye (earth), you existed in Orun (the spiritual realm) as part of a community. You weren't alone. You had relationships. You made agreements about what this lifetime would be, what you'd experience, what you'd learn, who you'd meet, what you'd contribute.

Your Egbe witnessed all of it. It saw you choose your destiny. Some of them agreed to come with you (those are the people you meet in life who feel like you've always known them). Others stayed in Orun.

What Egbe Does (And How You've Already Experienced Them)

Your Egbe holds the memory of who you really are and what you came here to do. While you're down here navigating amnesia (the forgetting that comes with birth), it remembers everything. It orchestrates synchronicities, arranges encounters with the right people at the right time, open doors when you're in alignment and close doors when you're drifting off course. It sends signs, creates friction when necessary, and smooths the path when you're living in accordance with your agreements. It witnesses your life.

Everything you do here in Aiye is seen by your Egbe in Orun. Your successes matter to it. Your struggles matter to it. You're not just living for yourself. You are the earthly expression of a collective that's invested in your journey.

You've experienced your Egbe even if you've never heard the word before. It shows up as the person you meet who feels instantly familiar, like you've known them for lifetimes. That's because you have. They're part of your soul group who incarnated alongside you.

It shows up in patterns that keep recurring regardless of how you try to change them. Those aren't accidents or punishments. They're soul agreements still active, trying to get your attention.

It shows up when you think of someone and they call five minutes later. When you need an answer and a book falls off the shelf. When you're at a crossroads and a stranger says exactly what you needed to hear.

It shows up in your dreams, especially recurring dreams or dreams where you're in places that feel more real than waking life. That's you visiting Orun, checking in with your soul group while your body sleeps.

It shows up when doors close in your face no matter how hard you push. That's not the universe being cruel. That's your Egbe redirecting you because that path doesn't align with what you actually agreed to.

It shows up when something clicks into place so easily it feels like magic. When the job appears out of nowhere. When the money shows up right on time. When the relationship that's meant for you finds you without effort. That's orchestration.

When Egbe Orchestrates: The "We Clan" Recognition

One of the running jokes in my friend group is "We clan." It's what we say when we're describing someone who fits right in or we discover (again) that we've been on parallel paths without knowing it. I don't remember when we started saying it as a playful acknowledgment that we're more than friends, we're soul family who found each other in this lifetime. It stuck because it's true.

We'll share what we've been processing spiritually, and realize we've all been getting the same downloads, navigating the same challenges, receiving the same clarity at the exact same time. We laugh about it. "We clan," we say. But it's not actually a joke. And it's never coincidence.

It's Egbe.

When soul groups incarnate together, they stay connected across the veil. When one member is ready for a particular lesson or breakthrough, the entire group gets activated. The orchestration isn't happening at the human level. We're not consciously coordinating. It's happening in Orun, where our Egbe is in constant coordination of our agreements, and it filters down into Aiye through what we call synchronicity.

I've learned to work with this intentionally.

I have a prayer I say, especially when I need things to flow smoothly, when I'm navigating bureaucracy, when I'm walking into situations where I need support: "May everyone I run into today be a part of my Egbe."

When I'm dealing with paperwork that could go either way, when I'm sitting across from someone who has the power to approve or deny what I need, when I'm in spaces where the outcome depends on someone else's decision, I pray that the person whose desk I land at, the person who says my name, the person who makes the call, is part of my Egbe.

Because if they are? Everything changes. They're going to try to work with me. They're not going to be against me, even if they don't consciously know why. Suddenly what should have been difficult becomes surprisingly easy. The paperwork gets pushed through. The exception gets made. The door that was supposed to be closed somehow opens.

That's not manipulation. That's alignment.

What I'm asking for isn't control over outcomes or forcing situations to go my way. I'm asking for resonance. I'm asking that if there's someone in my soul group positioned to support what I'm here to do, that we find each other in that moment.

And it works, not because I'm special, but because that's how soul groups function. We're designed to support each other's agreements. When two members of the same Egbe connect in Aiye, there's a natural inclination toward collaboration, toward making things work, toward supporting the path.

You've experienced this, even if you didn't have language for it.

The job interview that felt like talking to an old friend, where the conversation flowed so easily you almost forgot it was an interview. The stranger at the coffee shop who overheard your conversation and offered exactly the resource you needed, then disappeared before you could properly thank them. That was orchestration. That was your soul group arranging an encounter to deliver information at the exact moment you needed it.

The person who went out of their way to help you for no logical reason, who spent extra time, who broke protocol, who made an exception they "normally wouldn't make." That was their Egbe responding to yours, even if neither of you consciously understood what was happening.

This is how soul groups work across the veil. They arrange circumstances. They position people. They create moments of resonance that feel like luck or coincidence or being in the right place at the right time.

But it's not random. It's orchestrated.

"We clan" isn't just a cute saying. It's recognition of a spiritual reality: some of us came here together, agreed to support each other's paths, and are living out those agreements whether we consciously remember them or not.

When you find your people (the ones who feel like home, the ones you don't have to explain yourself to, the ones who understand the work you're here to do without you having to justify it), you haven't just found friends. You've found your Egbe incarnated.

That recognition is precious. Honor it. Protect it. And trust that your soul group is orchestrating more connections like that, more moments of resonance, more encounters that feel like remembering.

Because that's exactly what they are. You're not meeting new people. You're recognizing old souls. You're not building community. You're remembering the community you've always belonged to.

And the more you align with your agreements, the more these connections will find you. Your Egbe will make sure of it.

Understanding "Egbe Is You": Resolving the Paradox

This is where people get confused. I want to address it directly because these are questions I get often when I start trying to explain Egbe:

"If Egbe is me, why am I talking TO them? If they're an aspect of my consciousness, why does it feel like they're external? How can Egbe be 'me' but also 'in Orun while I'm in Aiye'?"

Let me clarify what "Egbe is you" actually means.

Your consciousness is bigger than this body, this personality, this lifetime.

Imagine you're playing a video game. You're fully immersed in the game, controlling your character, navigating the landscape, making decisions within the game world. That's you in Aiye: incarnated, in a body, experiencing time and space and limitation.

Your Egbe is you as the player outside the game. You see the bigger map. You know the mission objectives. You can coordinate with other players. You have access to information the character in the game doesn't have.

The character IS you. The player IS you. But they're operating at different levels of awareness.

Both are you. They're just functioning in different dimensions.

When I say 'talk to your Egbe,' you're communicating between the limited-awareness part of you (in a body, in time, in Aiye) and the expanded-awareness part of you (in the field, beyond time, in Orun).

This is why Egbe work sometimes feels like talking to yourself and sometimes feels like receiving guidance from something bigger.

Because it's both.

You're talking to yourself. The bigger, eternal, collective version of yourself.

Another way to think about it: Your consciousness is like an ocean. You, reading this book right now, are a wave. You're a distinct, recognizable form with your own movement, your own expression, your own temporary identity. But you're not separate from the ocean. You're made of ocean. You ARE ocean, just in wave form.

Your Egbe is the ocean. More precisely: Your Egbe is the part of your consciousness that remains in the infinite field (Orun) while another part of your consciousness incarnates here (Aiye).

The Individual and the Collective

The next layer: Your individual eternal self (what we call Enikeji Orun in Yoruba cosmology) is part of your Egbe.

You are an individuated soul. You have your own essence, your own journey, your own unique expression. That's your Enikeji Orun.

But your Enikeji Orun belongs to a collective. A soul family. A group of consciousness that shares resonance, purpose, agreements. That's your Egbe.

Egbe is the collective consciousness you belong to. Enikeji Orun is the individuated consciousness you are. Both are you, just at different levels of awareness.

When you connect with your Egbe, you're not connecting with "other beings." You're connecting with your spiritual family. And since your Enikeji Orun (which is you) is embedded in that family, it can feel like you're connecting with yourself. You are. And you're also connecting with your kin.

Why the Language Feels Contradictory

Throughout this book, I talk about Egbe as "it," a singular entity. But I've also said Egbe is a collective, a group, a society. So which is it?

Both.

Egbe is a collective consciousness that functions as a unified field. Think of it like an orchestra: many instruments, one sound. Many souls, one Egbe. The collective operates as a single entity in relationship to you.

This isn't a contradiction to "Egbe is you."

Your Egbe is the expanded-awareness version of your own consciousness. The collective field your individual soul belongs to. When I say "your Egbe orchestrates" or "it sends signs" or "it witnessed your choices," I'm talking about the part of YOU that exists in Orun.

You're not separate from your Egbe any more than a wave is separate from the ocean.

What My Godmother Taught Me

Years into my journey with Egbe, my godmother told me something that shifted everything.

I was asking questions about all this elaborate ritual work, trying to connect with my Egbe, making offerings, saying prayers, basically doing all the things. And, not in these words, but her sentiment was definitely, "You're doing too much."

I was confused. Wasn't I supposed to be honoring them? Wasn't I supposed to be building the relationship?

She put her hand on the crown of her head and said, "They are an aspect of you. If all you have is yourself, all you need to do is connect with yourself and connect with the earth."

It was so simple, but it cracked something open in me.

What she was saying is that Egbe isn't something far away from you, something external that you have to reach for. Egbe is woven into the fabric of who you are. Not as the eternal individual self, but as the collective consciousness your soul belongs to. It's the group aspect of your eternal nature.

Both are you. Just in different dimensions.

You can make ritual if you want to. You can say prayers and make offerings and create beautiful space. But you don't need an elaborate ceremony to connect with your Egbe. All you need is presence and your willingness to recognize what's always been there.

Put your hand on your head. Breathe. Connect with the earth beneath you. And know that your Egbe is right there, because it has never left.

The Reciprocal Relationship

There's a prayer I say often that I learned from an elder, one that captures the essence of this reciprocal relationship: "Egbe, please do not let me be an embarrassment here on earth."

That phrase captures the essence of this relationship. You're asking your soul group to support you in Orun so that you can be a good reflection of them in Aiye. It's reciprocal.

When you honor it (through offerings, prayers, living in alignment with your agreements), it honors you by orchestrating favorable circumstances.

When Egbe is good in Orun, life is sweet in Aiye. When you neglect it, when you live in opposition to what you agreed to, when you refuse the path your soul chose, life gets hard. Not as punishment, but as redirection.

This is correspondence in action: as above, so below. What you do here affects them there. What they do there affects you here. You're not separate from your Egbe. You're its presence in physical form.

This Isn't Just Isese

I want to be clear about something. Egbe Orun is an Isese teaching, part of the traditional spiritual practice of the Yoruba cosmology. It comes from a specific lineage, with specific language, rituals, and cosmology. I was initiated into this tradition, and I honor the ancestors who carried this knowledge through centuries of upheaval, colonization, and spiritual suppression.

But my work with Egbe has shown me this: The Yoruba were not describing something unique to their culture. They were describing how consciousness works.

And that truth traveled.

Even when Yoruba people were forcibly displaced during the Maafa and the Trans-Atlantic Slave Trade, the spiritual technologies they carried

(Egbe, Ori, ancestral continuity, spiritual agreements) did not vanish. They re-rooted themselves throughout the diaspora: in Lucumí in Cuba, Candomblé in Brazil, Trinidad Orisa, Shango Baptist, Oyotunji, and countless blended or re-emergent traditions. The outward expressions changed. The inner architecture remained.

And it's not just in the diaspora.

Every spiritual tradition I've studied has some version of this teaching. Soul families. Star seeds. Bodhisattva groups. Monads. The Council of Elders. In Western metaphysics, they talk about soul contracts and pre-birth agreements. In Buddhism, karmic groups reincarnate together. In Christian mysticism, there's the communion of saints, a spiritual collective that transcends physical life.

The details differ. The rituals differ. The cultural framing differs. But the underlying truth is consistent: You didn't come here alone. You made agreements before incarnation.

And there is a collective consciousness, your soul group, that holds those agreements and supports your evolution.

I use the Yoruba framework because that is the system that gave me language for something my soul already knew. But nothing in this book requires you to formally work with Egbe by name.

If you resonate with the idea of soul groups, if you sense that you have a spiritual family across lifetimes, if you feel guided or supported by something beyond your individual self, then you are already in relationship with your Egbe. You just may be calling it something else.

The Part No One Tells You

When you come to Aiye, you forget. Not completely, but enough that the memory of your soul group becomes something you feel rather than something you consciously know.

That forgetting isn't a mistake. It's how you fully commit to being here. If you remembered everything, you'd never stop looking over your shoulder, wanting to go back.

So yes, you'll have moments where something in you aches for what you cannot name. Moments where you feel a longing for a place you've never visited in this lifetime. Where you look around at your life and think, *This is good, but it's not... everything.* This isn't dysfunction. It's memory trying to surface. It's your soul recognizing what it once knew before the veil of incarnation settled over you.

But your Egbe in Orun? They remember everything.

They remember who you are, what you came here to do, what you agreed to experience. And they're constantly working behind the scenes to help you live out those agreements.

Why This Matters

Understanding Egbe changes everything about how you navigate your life. You stop seeing obstacles as bad luck and start recognizing them as course corrections. You stop forcing doors that won't open and start trusting that closed doors are protection. You stop feeling alone in your journey and start sensing the support that's been there all along.

You begin to recognize that the quiet pull you've always felt (the sense that there's something more, something you can't quite name) isn't confusion or dissatisfaction. It's the echo of your agreements. It's your Egbe reminding you of who you are and what you came here to do.

And you understand that you're not here to figure this out alone. You have a whole spiritual collective behind you, orchestrating, witnessing, remembering, supporting. Your work isn't to earn their help. You just need to align with what your Egbe already knows is true.

This shifts how you approach spiritual practice entirely. When you make offerings to Egbe, you're not bribing external entities. Instead, you're creating energetic reciprocity between different dimensions of your own being. When you pray to Egbe, you're not begging for help; you're communicating across the veil of incarnation, reconnecting with what you already know at the soul level. When you ask Egbe for guidance, you're not waiting for messages from outside yourself. You're tuning into the part of your own consciousness that sees the bigger picture.

This is spiritual sovereignty. You're not dependent on external forces to save you, fix you, or guide you. You're learning to access the parts of yourself that already know the way. Your Egbe isn't out there somewhere, separate from you, deciding whether or not to help. Your Egbe is you, remembering what you chose before you forgot, orchestrating from the dimension where forgetting doesn't exist.

The work isn't to reach them. The work is to remember that you never left.

PART 3: THE FRAMEWORK YOU NEED

Now that you understand what Egbe is (your soul group, the part of you that exists in Orun while you navigate Aiye), I need to show you the framework that explains HOW this actually works.

You'll see the nuance of how your Egbe influences your life and why certain spiritual principles show up across every tradition on earth. For me, this is the crux of the entire book. If you understand this, everything else will make sense.

The Law of Correspondence: "As Above, So Below"

After my initiation, I started doing Ose Egbe, a regular observance to connect with my Egbe. Weekly, I would set time aside with offerings such as sugarcane, sweets, fruit, kola nut, sometimes toys or small childlike items, ekuru, and honey, along with simple prayers. These offerings are given to Egbe to acknowledge their presence, refresh them, and maintain harmony. The purpose of Ose Egbe is to let them know you remember them here in Aiye and to build connection between you and your spiritual companions.

There's a universal principle that shows up across spiritual traditions, mystery schools, and indigenous cosmologies around the world. In Hermetic philosophy, it's called the Law of Correspondence.

The principle is simple: **As above, so below. As within, so without.**

What exists in the spiritual realm mirrors what exists in the physical realm. What exists inside your consciousness manifests in your external circumstances. The microcosm reflects the macrocosm. The individual soul reflects the universal consciousness.

This isn't metaphor. This is mechanics.

Everything that exists in Aiye (the physical world you can see, touch, and measure) has a corresponding reality in Orun, the spiritual realm. Every person walking around in a body has a spiritual counterpart. Every choice you make here ripples there. Every agreement you hold there influences what unfolds here.

You are not split between these two realms. You exist in both simultaneously.

You Are a Multidimensional Being

Right now, as you read these words, you exist in multiple dimensions at once.

There's the physical you, the person sitting here with a body, breathing, thinking, feeling. That's you in Aiye.

And there's the spiritual you, the consciousness that exists beyond physical form, the part of you that has always existed and will continue to exist after this body is done. That's you in Orun.

Most people think of these as separate states. Like you're here in the physical world and your soul is somewhere "up there" waiting for you to die so you can reunite with it.

That's not how it works.

You are not split. You are simultaneous.

The part of you in Aiye and the part of you in Orun are the same consciousness operating at different frequencies. One hasn't forgotten. One remembers everything. But they're both you.

Think back to the video game metaphor I shared earlier. You're the character in the game AND the player outside the game. Both are you, operating at different levels of awareness.

Or think of it like standing in a room with two mirrors on opposite walls. One mirror shows your physical reflection, what you look like in form. The other mirror shows your energetic reflection, the frequency you're emitting, the agreements you're holding, the consciousness you're operating from.

You're not choosing between the mirrors. You're standing in both reflections at once.

That's what it means to exist in Aiye and Orun simultaneously.

How Egbe Works Through Correspondence

Now this is where Egbe comes in more clearly.

Your Egbe knows:

- What you chose to learn
- The gifts you committed to using
- The people you agreed to meet
- The challenges you said you were ready to face
- The purpose you came here to fulfill

They don't hold this information about you. They hold it as you. Because they're the part of your consciousness that exists where forgetting doesn't happen.

This is why the Law of Correspondence matters so much. What your Egbe knows in Orun (above) directly influences what unfolds in your life in Aiye (below). What you believe and feel and choose in Aiye (within) creates the frequency that determines what your Egbe can orchestrate for you in Orun (without).

As above, so below. As within, so without.

It's not one-directional. It's not your Egbe pulling strings while you passively experience the results. It's a constant feedback loop between the part of you that remembers and the part of you that's learning to remember.

Your Frequency Activates Your Agreements

Pre-birth agreements are not fate. They are activated by your current consciousness.

You made agreements before you came into this lifetime, that's true. But those agreements don't unfold automatically. They unfold when your frequency matches the agreement.

In Yoruba cosmology, there's a saying: "Nothing can happen to you if your Ori will not allow it."

Your Ori is your inner consciousness: your beliefs, your frequency, your energetic signature in this present moment. It's the aspect of you that has the power to say yes or no to what your soul agreed to.

If your mouth says "I want abundance" but your Ori (your beliefs, your frequency, your deep internal programming) says "I'm not worthy," your Ori wins. Every time.

Your Egbe can orchestrate opportunities, synchronicities, encounters, and doorways. But you have to walk through them. You have to be energetically aligned enough to recognize them. You have to do the internal work that shifts your frequency into resonance with what you said you wanted before you got here.

This is why spiritual work matters. This is why healing trauma, clearing limiting beliefs, and doing the inner work of becoming who you actually are isn't optional. It's how you activate your agreements.

Your Egbe isn't making things happen TO you. Your Egbe is orchestrating circumstances that match what you're energetically committed to, not what you're saying you want, but what your Ori is actually broadcasting.

When those two align, when what you're saying matches what you're believing, when your frequency rises to meet your soul agreements, that's when everything starts moving.

That's what orchestration actually looks like.

This Is Not Spiritual Bypassing

Understanding Egbe and pre-birth agreements is not permission to avoid responsibility for your life.

It's not: "Well, I chose this suffering before I was born, so I guess I just have to accept it."

It's: "I chose certain lessons and growth edges before I was born, AND I have the power right now to do the healing work that transforms how those lessons show up."

Your agreements aren't punishments. They're not karmic debts you're paying off. They're not evidence that you're being tested by some external force.

They're the curriculum you chose because your soul knew it was ready for that level of growth.

And the empowering part: you get to decide how you move through that curriculum. You can do it the hard way, resisting, denying, repeating the same patterns over and over. Or you can do it the aligned way, leaning into the lessons, doing the healing work, allowing your frequency to shift so that your external circumstances can shift too.

Your Egbe orchestrates based on your frequency. Change your frequency, and the orchestration changes.

That's not abdication. That's accountability.

What This Means for Your Daily Life

When you understand the Law of Correspondence and how Egbe works through it, you start seeing your life differently.

When doors close repeatedly, you recognize this isn't aligned with what you agreed to; your Egbe is redirecting you.

When synchronicities stack up, when the right people appear, when opportunities materialize, when things flow with surprising ease, you recognize you're in alignment. Your frequency matches your agreements.

When certain people trigger you repeatedly, you recognize this is showing you something unhealed. This pattern is here because there's work to do.

When you feel that pull toward something you can't explain (a move, a career change, a relationship ending, a creative project), you recognize your Egbe is orchestrating. Your soul remembers something your mind hasn't caught up to yet.

Your life becomes the feedback system. Your Egbe creates the circumstances. Your Ori (your current consciousness) determines how you respond. And the correspondence between what's happening in Orun and what's happening in Aiye becomes visible.

You're not a victim of your soul agreements. You're the living bridge between the dimension where you made them and the dimension where you're fulfilling them.

But understanding Egbe raises another question: Who exactly is doing the choosing? Who is witnessing? And who carries it all forward?

REFLECTION QUESTIONS

Before you move forward, take time to sit with these questions:

1. Have you ever felt like there's a part of you that exists somewhere else, watching your life unfold? Like you're both living your life AND witnessing it at the same time?
2. Where in your life have you experienced moments of perfect timing that felt too orchestrated to be random?
3. What have you always known that you couldn't explain?
4. Now that you understand Egbe is you (the expanded-consciousness version of you), how does that change how you think about spiritual guidance, synchronicities, and soul agreements?

CHAPTER 2

THE ENIKEJI ORUN: YOUR ETERNAL SOUL SELF

You've met your Egbe. You understand it witnesses your agreements, orchestrates your circumstances, holds your truth when you forget it. But who made the agreements they're witnessing? Who chose this life? Who carries the pattern across lifetimes?

If Egbe are my heavenly companions, the ones I share destiny with, then who was the "I" they were connected to? What part of me existed in Orun with them before I was born, and what part of me is here now, trying to live out whatever we agreed to?

These questions wouldn't let me go.

Everyone kept saying, "Egbe are your spiritual mates," "They're your heavenly companions," "You have a soul group in Orun." I'd learned about the different classes: Iyalode, Eleeko, Jagunjagun, and their various attributes. Each class has different characteristics (Iyalode are leaders, Jagunjagun are warriors), but understanding your specific class isn't required to work with Egbe. What matters is recognizing the relationship itself. The information was there. But I kept circling around one question: How do they actually connect to me?

The Orisa are universal forces. Yemoja is Yemoja whether she's working with me or someone else. Shango is Shango. They're vast, archetypal, collective. You approach them, honor them, work with them, but they're not yours in any personal sense.

But Egbe felt different.

Ori felt different.

My connection to Ifa felt different.

These three were mine. Personal. Intimate. Not shared across hundreds of practitioners, but specific to my journey, my choices, my path.

That realization (that Ori, Ifa, and Egbe were personal to me in a way the Orisa weren't) meant I needed to go deeper. I needed to understand not just what Egbe are, but how they functioned in relationship to me specifically. How they connected to my destiny. How they related to the choices I'd made before I got here.

The Search for Understanding

After my initiation, I was thirsty for knowledge. I have a compulsion for understanding new concepts that sometimes borders on obsession. I exist in this constant balance: trying to let things exist and unravel in spirit (faith) while simultaneously trying to silence the thinking part of my brain that feels like it must absolutely make sense of something.

I read everything I could find. I went through Ayo Salami's book multiple times, taking notes, trying to understand the cosmology. I asked questions of every elder who would talk to me. I sat with the confusion, wrestling with concepts I couldn't quite articulate, but I knew there was something I was supposed to get that hadn't clicked yet.

I kept hitting the same walls and coming back to the same questions. You know how you can be in a conversation with someone and you're trying to understand something, but you aren't even sure what you're trying to understand? And the questions became circular. That was me trying to understand Egbe. I was reading, and learning, and living, and yet I knew there was something I still wasn't grasping.

It wasn't until I discovered the Akashic Records that I had a starting point to begin formulating the questions that would ultimately lead me to this work. (I'll tell you that story in Chapter 3. One of those perfectly timed synchronicities that could only have been Egbe orchestrating.)

But what about the eternal soul? What about past lives? What about the continuity of consciousness across multiple incarnations?

African Traditional Religions didn't emphasize reincarnation in the way I was encountering it in my Akashic Records work. And now, diving deeper into Isese practice, I wasn't finding clear answers about how the eternal soul fit with the Yoruba concepts of Ori and Egbe.

Then I found the concept of Enikeji Orun (or re-found, but this time with the right question).

It was like someone had handed me the missing puzzle piece.

Enikeji Orun. I understood it as the individuated soul self, and later, through my questioning and unraveling, came to know it as the eternal soul self: the aspect of me that exists in Orun across all lifetimes, not just this one. The individuated thread that carries my essence from incarnation to incarnation.

And suddenly, I could see how it all fit together.

Egbe wasn't just my soul mates. It was the collective consciousness my eternal soul belongs to, the collective that includes and surrounds my Enikeji Orun. It witnesses not just what I chose in this incarnation, but what I've been choosing across multiple incarnations. Based on those choices, my Egbe for each lifetime is determined.

There was no conflict between Yoruba cosmology and universal metaphysics. I just needed to expand the lens through which I was looking. They were describing the same reality from different angles.

That's when I stopped searching and started integrating.

Wait, So Who Actually Chose My Destiny?

By the end of this chapter, you'll be able to hold this
simple framework:
Ori = destiny selector for this lifetime
Egbe = witness and support team for this lifetime
Enikeji Orun = eternal carrier across all lifetimes
But first, let's break down how we got here.

If you've spent any time studying or reading about Egbe, you might have hit a confusing wall. On one hand, you hear that Egbe are the ones you "share destiny with," the ones who hold your spiritual agreements. On the other hand, you hear about Ori, your inner head, your personal deity, as the one who chooses your destiny before you're born.

So which is it? Did your Egbe decide what you'd experience in this life? Or did your Ori?

The answer: When your Ori chose your destiny, your Egbe saw it.

What the Enikeji Orun Actually Is

The Enikeji Orun is often described as your "heavenly double," the part of you that remained in Orun when you incarnated into Aiye. And that's true.

But it's deeper than that.

Your Enikeji Orun is you. Not just the you of this lifetime, but the eternal, individuated aspect of your being that has existed across all your incarnations.

Your consciousness exists in two dimensions. In some versions of Yoruba cosmology, Olodumare breathes *emi* (life force) into the soul before it chooses its Ori. In others, the Ori chooses first, then receives the breath of life. What matters for our purposes is this: one part of your consciousness descended into Aiye in this body, and one part remained in Orun as your Enikeji Orun.

Your Enikeji Orun is not some separate spirit floating around. It's the rest of you. The part that didn't descend into density. The part that holds the memory of not just what you chose before this birth, but what you've been choosing across all your incarnations.

Understanding Enikeji Orun becomes richer when you see how it relates to concepts from other spiritual traditions, all pointing to the same truth: something eternal in you continues across lifetimes.

Different traditions describe the eternal soul differently. Some emphasize its creative, generative power: the divine spark actively shaping your path. Yoruba thought emphasizes its witnessing capacity: Enikeji Orun as the eternal thread carrying continuity. But across traditions, the core truths remain: the soul exists before birth, continues beyond death, plays a role in destiny, and requires your participation to fulfill what it chose.

Where Ifa Comes In

Ifa is the divination system we go to when we need to remember our destiny: the choices we made before we were born. When life gets confusing, when we've wandered off path, when we need clarity about what our Ori selected, we consult Ifa. Ifa reveals what was chosen. Egbe helps us live it. And Enikeji Orun holds the memory of why we chose it in the first place.

When your Ori said, "This is what I choose to experience," your Egbe said, "We see what you've chosen, and here's how we can help." Ifa says, "Let me remind you what you chose." And your Enikeji Orun? Enikeji Orun is the eternal essence carrying all of this forward. Not just for this lifetime, but across all lifetimes.

Holding It All Together

Now that you've seen how Ori, Egbe, and Enikeji Orun work together, this is how I hold all three:

Ori chose what lessons you'd learn THIS time around: the specific experiences, relationships, and challenges that would shape this incarnation. Ori sanctions.

Egbe witnessed those choices and agreed to help you live them out, both the members who incarnated alongside you and those who remained in Orun to orchestrate from the spiritual realm. They are your accountability partners.

Enikeji Orun remembers why you chose them. It has carried this wisdom across every lifetime you've ever lived, holding the thread of your eternal development. It's the eternal soul self.

You are all three.

You're not just one piece of this. You are the Ori that chose this lifetime's destiny, the Egbe that saw and supports it, and the Enikeji Orun that carries the eternal thread of who you've always been.

The Integration

This is why you can't fully understand Egbe without understanding Ori. And you can't understand your role in this life, or across lifetimes, without recognizing that you are the Enikeji Orun, that chose this particular Ori, that gathered this particular Egbe, and that carries it all forward through time.

You are not a victim of your destiny. You are the author of it.

And you're not alone in living it out.

But where does all of this exist? And how can you access it?

REFLECTION QUESTIONS

Before you move forward, take time to sit with these questions:

1. If you are the chooser (Ori), the witness (Egbe), and the eternal thread (Enikeji Orun) all at once, what does that change about how you see your life right now?
2. What have you been blaming on external forces that you actually chose?
3. When you think about your Enikeji Orun, the part of you that exists in Orun, what do you sense? What does that eternal aspect of you know that your human self has forgotten?

CHAPTER 3

THE AKASHIC RECORDS: WHERE EGBE, ENIKEJI, AND CONSCIOUSNESS MEET

How I Actually Found the Akashic Records

It was 2016, the year after my Egbe initiation. I'd been separated from my spouse for a few months, had just moved to Tallahassee to start my position at Florida State University, and I was in one of those life transitions where everything feels unstable and uncertain.

A friend in my group chat mentioned she'd gotten an Akashic Records reading. Then another friend did one. Then another. They kept talking about how transformative the experience was, how much clarity they'd received.

I'd never heard of the Akashic Records. But I was curious, and I needed guidance. So I booked a session.

The reader told me things about past lives that seemed completely absurd. Lives in other galaxies. Iterations of my soul that weren't even earth-based. Healing work I'd done across dimensions and time periods. My logical brain thought, "This is wild. What is happening?"

But what I couldn't dismiss: She also gave me incredibly concrete, accurate, verifiable information about my current life. Things she had no way of knowing. Patterns she named that I'd never articulated to anyone. Gifts she identified that I'd been hiding.

The combination of the far-out cosmic information and the undeniably accurate present-life information did something to me. I couldn't just write it off. So I sat with it. I let it be strange. I let it challenge everything I thought I knew about how souls work.

A year later, it was my birthday. I booked another reading. This time, the reader told me I had something called "soul loss" and that I needed to heal it.

I had no idea what soul loss was. I researched and found practitioners who could help, but they were expensive—way beyond what I could afford at the time.

A few days later, I was scrolling through my email, and I saw a subject line: "Heal Soul Loss."

I stopped. I had no memory of signing up for any email list related to Akashic Records. I had no idea how this email landed in my inbox.

But there it was. An offering to learn how to access the Akashic Records myself, and there was a module specifically about healing soul loss.

I took it as a sign. I enrolled in the class.

The teacher didn't use a prayer-based process like I teach now. She did an energetic attunement and taught us to trust the field, to access it through visualization and intention. Simple. Direct. No elaborate ritual.

I was skeptical. So I started practicing on friends, on anyone who would let me. And the information came through. Accurate. Specific. Helpful.

One practice session turned into another. Word spread. People started asking me for readings. What started as a personal healing tool became a practice. Then a skill. Then, eventually, my business.

CHI Healing Institute was born because I was trying to heal my own soul loss. Everything after that (the thousands of clients, the teaching, the Soul Blueprint readings, the books I wrote on the Akashic Records) came from that one synchronistic email that showed up exactly when I needed it.

Looking back now, I see Egbe's hand all over it. The friend group talking about Akashic Records. The email appearing at the perfect moment. The doors opening, one after another, without me forcing anything. That's what orchestration looks like when you're in alignment.

I thought the Akashic Records were one thing, and Egbe was another thing. Two separate systems.

It took years for me to see how they connect.

Why This Mattered Given My Background

I've been part of African traditional religious systems since 2000. I started in the Lucumí system, where I was first introduced to and studied the Orisa tradition, and shortly afterward I was initiated into Palo Mayombe. It wasn'tt until 2015, when I was told about initiation into Egbe, that I transitioned into the Isese tradition.

And in all that time, I had never encountered the language of soul groups, eternal souls carrying lessons across lifetimes, or pre-birth agreements in the way Western metaphysics describes them. Even though Yoruba cosmology acknowledges that souls continue to be born again, the idea of a continual life that retains memories and lessons (this concept of an eternal soul) was not familiar to me in the way it was being presented through the Records.

When I started working in the Akashic Records (really, when I had my first Akashic Records reading), everything began to shift.

What Are the Akashic Records?

Before I explain how the Records connect to Egbe, let me start with what they actually are.

The Akashic Records are often described as an infinite library, but that metaphor can be misleading. They're not shelves of books or filing cabinets in some celestial hall. The Records are an energetic field, a vibrational body of consciousness where every thought, choice, experience, and possibility from every soul across all lifetimes is stored.

The living memory of existence itself.

I wrote extensively about the Records in my book *Accessing the Akashic Records: A Practical Guide to Healing, Clarity, and Empowerment (2024)*, where I break down how to access this field for healing and soul-level understanding. What matters here is how the Records relate to Egbe and your eternal soul self.

Here's what you need to know: Every soul that has ever incarnated has left an imprint in this field. Every choice you've made, every emotion you've felt, every agreement you entered before birth, every lesson you came here to learn is archived in the Records. Not as judgment or punishment, but as information. As wisdom. As the soul-level view of your journey.

The Records hold both your personal archive and the collective memory of all consciousness. When you access them, you're tapping into your soul's specific journey while also connecting to the infinite field of universal knowing.

Soul Groups in Metaphysics and the Akashic Records

In metaphysical teachings and Akashic Records work, we often speak about soul groups as collectives of souls who incarnate together across lifetimes to support one another's growth. These are not random associations. Soul groups are spiritually aligned beings who share frequency, purpose, and agreements. They witness your pre-incarnation choices, support your journey through lifetimes, and help you remember what you came here to do.

Soul groups can show up as family members, close friends, teachers, or even brief but impactful encounters. They are the souls who feel familiar when you meet them, who challenge you in ways that force your growth, who show up in your dreams and meditations as witnesses to your path.

When you access the Akashic Records, soul group information often emerges. You begin to see patterns: souls you've incarnated with before, agreements you made with specific people, lessons you're learning together across time.

This concept of soul groups isn't unique to any one tradition. It shows up across spiritual systems because it points to a universal truth: you are part of a collective. You did not come here alone.

And this is where Egbe becomes essential.

Egbe = Soul Groups

Egbe is the Yoruba framework for understanding that you belong to a spiritual collective, that you are part of a peer group in Orun who witnessed your choices before you incarnated and continues to hold space for you as you navigate Aiye.

Egbe Orun is the culturally specific language for a universal principle. What we call "soul groups" in Akashic Records work, the Yoruba people have always called Egbe Orun.

Same truth. Different language.

The Moment I Realized They Were Connected

That was the spark. Once I began doing Akashic Records work myself, I was getting clients left and right. It was making me go deeper, and because I'm naturally curious, I was reading everything, studying all the books, going into my own Records, asking and researching, working with my Egbe. All of these things were coming together.

I don't think there was an exact moment where I thought, "Wait, these are the same things." It was more a slow unfolding of synchronicities and connections. Because my clientele started to include a lot of people who were practitioners of ATRs, I began to see these same patterns across different paths. I had clients from the Orisa community, the Akan tradition, Palo Mayombe, Sangomas…literally all types of traditions. People coming to me to deal with things that had been recurring issues, dreams that felt familiar, agreements that seemed to span lifetimes.

I remember working with a client who had been having persistent dreams of being by water with a group of people who felt like family, but weren't anyone she recognized from this lifetime. In her waking life, she struggled with chronic feelings of loneliness and displacement, despite being surrounded by loving people.

When I accessed her Records, the information that came through was about soul agreements, promises she had made with a specific group of souls before incarnating. Her loneliness wasn't dysfunction. It was her soul self remembering her spiritual family.

As I was explaining this to her, something clicked for me. I realized I was describing what Egbe does.

If soul groups witness your pre-incarnation choices in metaphysical terms, then Egbe witnesses your choices in Yoruba terms. If your soul-self carries agreements across lifetimes in Records language, then your Enikeji Orun carries agreements across lifetimes in Yoruba language. If the Records archive every soul's journey in universal terms, then Egbe relationships are archived in the same infinite field.

They weren't two separate systems. They were two ways of accessing the same truth.

What I Need You to Understand

I'm not saying my gifts exist because of Egbe. That would put us right back into spiritual dependency: the idea that you need initiation, need specific practices, need external forces to access your own soul-level truth. And that's not what this book is about.

My natural soul gift, the thing I've had since before any initiation, is the ability to access and receive information from other dimensions and realms. I'm claircognizant. I just know things. I've always been this way.

What the Egbe initiation did was heighten that gift. Initiation doesn't bring new gifts. It awakens what's already there. It brings you into alignment with aspects of yourself, reminds you of agreements, clears blockages, brings dormant capacities to the forefront.

While everyone has Egbe in some form, not everyone is called to live as a child of Egbe. For those whose primary soul group is Egbe and who are called into that relationship through initiation, a common trait is this ability to move multidimensionally. To receive information across realms. To access soul-level truth with ease.

But the gift was already mine. The initiation just turned up the volume.

Now let me explain how this connects to the Akashic Records and why understanding this relationship matters.

The Unified Field (Universal Consciousness)

Imagine the largest possible container. Everything that exists, every thought, every soul, every experience across all dimensions and timelines, is held within this infinite field of consciousness.

I call it the "big bowl of galactic soup." Everything is just floating around in there. All information. All possibilities. All of it, right now, accessible.

But if we had to navigate that infinite field directly, it would be overwhelming. Too vast. Too unfiltered. We'd get lost.

The Akashic Records (The Organized Subset)

The Akashic Records are a subset of that larger unified field. They pull all that infinite information into an organized system we can actually access and work with.

Think of it like this: the unified field is the entire internet. The Akashic Records are a search engine that helps you find what you're looking for within that infinite data stream.

The Records give us a lens, a soul-level perspective, that allows us to access specific information in a way that makes sense to human consciousness. They organize the infinite into something navigable.

Egbe (The Keepers of Soul-Level Truth)

And Egbe? Egbe exists within that universal field as *Irunmole*, primordial consciousness that was there at the beginning. They hold soul-level truth. Not just for you, but as a function of what they are.

Now, depending on the lineage or background someone comes from, how they classify Egbe varies. Some regions within Nigeria speak of Egbe Orun as a group of spirits. Others relate to them more like Orisa. Some practitioners position them differently entirely.

I experience and work with Egbe as Irunmole, primordial consciousness that existed before the Orisa were specified, before creation took its current form. This isn't about one classification being "right" and others being "wrong." It's about recognizing that different lineages emphasize different aspects of the same truth.

What matters is this: Egbe holds soul-level authority. It was there when you made your agreements. It witnessed your Ori's choices. And it carries that memory forward, regardless of what you call them.

When I access the Akashic Records and read for clients, what I'm seeing when I look at agreements, soul patterns, and the eternal self is information held within that organized field.

When I access the Akashic Records of a client, what I'm actually doing, through a Yoruba cosmology lens, is accessing the memories and knowing of the Enikeji Orun. But understanding *why* this came so naturally to me took years.

The Relationship (Not the Dependency)

So this is the understanding:

- **Universal Consciousness** = The infinite field containing everything
- **Akashic Records** = The organized subset of that field, accessible through soul-level perspective
- **Egbe** = Primordial consciousness existing within the field, holders of soul-level truth
- **Your natural soul gifts** = What you came in with, what gets heightened through practice and initiation
- **Enikeji Orun** = The eternal soul self that exists in Orun, the "you" being accessed in the Records

One of the persistent questions during my initial venture into Akashic Records work was, "Why am I so good at this? Why is this natural?" This kept making me try to make sense of it all. Understanding Egbe from this larger cosmic lens is the thing that finally made it make sense.

This matters because I don't want you thinking you need Egbe initiation to access your soul-level truth. You don't. You need presence. Practice. Willingness to develop the gifts you already have.

For me, Egbe initiation, Akashic Records training, and years of practice all converged to heighten what was already there. That's my path. Your path might look completely different.

The Breakthrough: Egbe as Irunmole

The breakthrough came when I finally understood what it means that Egbe is Irunmole.

In Yoruba cosmology, creation unfolded in movements of consciousness. The Orisa are powerful forces within that structure. Before them came the Irunmole, the primordial energies present at the beginning when Olodumare first activated consciousness into existence.

Egbe is Irunmole. It was there at the start. Before time. Before form. Before any of this.

And if Egbe existed at the beginning of everything, that means it has access to EVERYTHING: all past, present, and future possibilities across every timeline, dimension, and soul record in every incarnation.

It's not magic. It's not special. It's just that when you're connected to Irunmole consciousness, you're connected to the part of the Universal Field that was there when the Records were being written.

That's why Egbe children (people deeply connected to their Egbe) tend to have prophetic gifts. We know things we shouldn't know. We see patterns others miss. We access information that seems to come from nowhere.

But the universal principle remains: everyone has access to soul-level truth. Everyone can connect with their eternal self. Everyone exists within the same unified field.

The tools and traditions are just different doorways into the same reality.

My curiosity about this connection didn't come out of nowhere. Through my teaching and training program, I certify people in the Akashic Records. I've taught hundreds of students, and among those who were Isese practitioners, the ones who took to the Records instantly and almost effortlessly were always the ones who had also been initiated into Egbe. I noticed the pattern long before I understood the reason.

And that pattern is part of what pushed me to keep asking questions.

Once I understood that Egbe is Irunmole consciousness (a consciousness present at the inception point of creation) the Akashic piece made sense. The

Akashic Records are the library. Egbe is part of the primordial intelligence that remembers how the library was built.

This explained why my access felt so clear and unobstructed.

I stopped treating them as separate systems and started seeing how they work together. Egbe holds my soul's truth. The Akashic Records hold the infinite field of all soul truth. My connection to Egbe helps me navigate that infinite field with ease.

That's the relationship. That's the connection.

And once I understood it, my work exploded in ways I couldn't have predicted.

Water as Primordial Spiritual Substance

To understand why Irunmole consciousness is so profound, go back to the beginning.

Before solid earth existed, there was only Orun (sky realm) above and endless primordial water below. This wasn't ordinary water. It was the original spiritual substance, undifferentiated consciousness from which all form would emerge. Irunmole were there when the boundary between spiritual and physical was first being drawn.

When Olodumare tasked Obatala with creating land, Obatala descended from heaven on a golden chain, carrying a snail shell filled with sand and a hen. He poured the sand onto the primordial waters, and the hen scratched and spread it, creating the first solid ground—Ile-Ife, the spiritual center of Yorubaland.

This is why Irunmole consciousness existed before the Orisa: they were present when there was no separation between Orun and Aiye, when everything was still primordial water, undifferentiated spiritual substance holding infinite potential.

Water remembers this. Water still carries that original nature.

Water shows up across spiritual practices worldwide as a medium for communication with the unseen; not because different cultures independently invented the same symbol, but because water's properties ARE what they represent. Water flows between states. Water holds memory. Water connects what appears separate.

When you offer water to your Egbe, you're not performing a symbolic gesture. You're working with the very substance that existed at creation, the element that bridges Orun and Aiye because it predates their separation.

Water is the primordial spiritual element. It's what existed when Irunmole consciousness was all there was: before land, before form, before the differentiation that created the world as we know it.

That's why simple water offerings are so powerful. You're not just giving liquid. You're offering the original spiritual substance, acknowledging the consciousness that existed before creation, working with the element that still remembers when everything was One.

Egbe in Everyday Life

Something else to think about: everything has Egbe. All things express collective consciousness, all part of larger communities that extend beyond what we can see. This means we're constantly interacting with Egbe, whether we realize it or not.

When you walk through a forest and feel that sense of ancient presence, you're not imagining it. You're sensing the collective consciousness of that ecosystem: the Egbe of the trees, the land, the spirits that tend that space. When you stand by the ocean and feel simultaneously small and connected, you're experiencing the soul group of water recognizing something in you.

And when you interact with other people? You're not just engaging with their individual personality or their human identity. You're engaging with their Egbe.

Think about it from a practical standpoint. You already exist as part of multiple groups in your everyday life. You're part of a family. You're part of a friendship circle. You're part of a professional community, a creative community, a spiritual community. You might be a parent in one space, a mentor in another, a student somewhere else, and a leader in yet another.

Each of those roles places you inside a different circle of people, responsibilities, and energy. Egbe works the same way.

Your Egbe in Orun is never just one group. You exist within multiple Egbe collectives at all times. Concentric circles of purpose, resonance, talent, destiny, and soul agreements. When I say, "I'm a teacher," that's an Egbe. "I'm a dancer," that's another Egbe. "I'm an author," another. "I'm a healer, a guide, a creator." Each of these identities reflects a different spiritual collective my soul is connected to.

The same is true for you.

You are part of many Egbe. Not one singular, fixed group, but an ecosystem of resonant collectives that reflect the different dimensions of who you are.

When you see someone else and offer them food, when you stop to help a stranger, when you acknowledge another person's dignity and humanity, that's not just a 3D action. I offer that this can be a way to acknowledge their Egbe and simultaneously acknowledge your own. It's recognizing the spiritual collectives they belong to, creating a moment of alignment that ripples into both Orun and Aiye.

In Sanskrit traditions, there's the greeting "Namaste," which means "I bow to the divine in you." The gesture acknowledges that we're all expressions of the same source, temporarily housed in separate forms. Recognizing the Egbe connection with someone else is a similar act.

One of my favorite sayings comes in response to the question, "How many Egbe are there?" The answer: "As many as there are grains of sand." This highlights that we could never conceive of how many groups exist because everything has Egbe. And these groups are constantly overlapping and operating concentrically within each other.

Two Languages, One Field

What I saw once the pieces came together:

In Yoruba cosmology, we speak of Egbe, your soul group in Orun who saw your pre-birth agreements and supports your journey in Aiye. In metaphysical teachings, we speak of soul groups, collectives of souls who incarnate together across lifetimes to support one another's growth.

Both describe the same reality. You belong to a spiritual collective. You made agreements before birth. Those agreements are being supported by beings who exist in the non-physical realm.

In Yoruba cosmology, we speak of Enikeji Orun, your eternal soul self that exists in Orun while you inhabit Aiye. In metaphysical teachings, we speak of the higher self, the soul self, the eternal aspect of consciousness that reincarnates across lifetimes. Both describe the same reality. There is a part of you that is eternal, that carries memory across incarnations, that exists beyond the limitations of this single lifetime.

In Yoruba cosmology, we speak of Orun, the spiritual realm where all souls originate and return. In metaphysical teachings, we speak of the unified field, Source consciousness, the infinite field, the Akash, Universal Mind. Both describe the same reality. There is a dimension of existence where all information lives, where all souls are connected, where every choice and agreement is held.

Different cultures. Different languages. Same truth.

Why do different cultures have different languages for the same truth? Because each tradition emerged from a specific relationship with consciousness. Yoruba cosmology developed in a culture that understood reciprocity, community, and ancestral continuity as foundational. Western metaphysics emerged from individualist cultures, so it emphasizes the individual soul. Neither is wrong. Both are true. And when you understand both, you get a richer, more complete picture.

The Field Where It All Lives

Whether you call it Orun, the Akash, Universal Consciousness, the Universe, or the Infinite Field, all of these words point to the same reality: a dimension of existence that holds everything.

Every thought. Every choice. Every soul. Every agreement. Every lifetime.

This field is not separate from you. It's not "out there" somewhere, accessible only to the spiritually advanced. You are part of this field.

You've always been part of it. Your Enikeji Orun exists within it right now, even as you read these words.

Your human self lives in Aiye, navigating physical reality, making choices, learning lessons. Your Enikeji Orun exists in Orun, connected to your Egbe, holding the eternal thread of who you are across all lifetimes. And both of these aspects of you exist within the infinite field of consciousness itself.

You are the wave and the ocean at the same time.

Accessing the Field

You might be wondering: How do I actually connect with this field? How do I access Orun, the Akashic Records, this infinite consciousness we've been discussing?

The truth is, you're already connected. You've never been disconnected. Your Enikeji Orun exists in this field right now. The question isn't whether you have access. It's whether you're paying attention.

When I first accessed the Akashic Records, I realized I wasn't reaching something far away. I was learning to recognize what was already present. It felt like tuning a radio. The signal was always broadcasting. I just needed to find the right frequency.

Accessing the field feels like this: It's the moment of knowing something you have no logical way of knowing. It's the clarity that arrives when you finally get still enough to hear it. It's the dream that feels more real than waking life. It's the synchronicity so precise it makes you laugh. It's the creative download that arrives fully formed. It's the wisdom that speaks through you when you're teaching, writing, or simply being present with someone who needs exactly what you carry.

Some people access this field through formal practice: Ifa divination, Akashic Records training, deep meditation, ceremonial work. Others access it through art, nature, movement, or spontaneous moments of clarity.

When you access the Records, you're not pulling information from some distant archive. You're accessing universal consciousness, within the infinite field that you're part of.

When you pray, meditate, receive divination, or simply know something you have no logical way of knowing, you're not connecting to something outside yourself. You're remembering what you already are.

You are consciousness experiencing itself in physical form. Your Egbe is the group consciousness you belong to. The infinite field is consciousness itself, the ground of all being, the source we all emerge from and return to.

There is no separation. There never was. The forgetting is part of the design, and the remembering is the journey.

Deepening Correspondence

Now that you understand the architecture, let's look at how this actually works in daily life.

How do you actually work with the Law of Correspondence? You pay attention to what's mirroring back to you. When doors close repeatedly, Correspondence may be showing you misalignment. When synchronicities stack up, Correspondence is confirming you're on path. When certain people trigger you, Correspondence is highlighting an opportunity to investigate unhealed agreements. Your life is the feedback system. Your Egbe is the one orchestrating it. And your Enikeji Orun is the one who can interpret the signals if you learn to listen.

When you're living in alignment with what your Ori chose, your external life reflects ease, flow, synchronicity. Doors open. The right people show up. Opportunities materialize. That's not luck. That's Correspondence. Your soul agreements in Orun are manifesting smoothly in Aiye because you're walking the path you chose.

When you're living out of alignment, when you're operating from societal conditioning, fear, or someone else's expectations instead of your soul's truth, your external life reflects friction, resistance, confusion. Doors close. Relationships fall apart. Nothing feels right. That's also

Correspondence. Your life is mirroring back to you that you've wandered off the path.

Your Egbe orchestrates circumstances to keep you aligned. Your Enikeji Orun sends signals through your intuition, your body, your dreams. Your life itself is the feedback system, constantly showing you whether you're living what you agreed to or living what you were taught to want.

The infinite field holds all of this. And you (your human self, your Enikeji Orun, your Egbe, all of it) are expressions of that field, experiencing itself through the journey of choice, consequence, and remembering.

REFLECTION QUESTIONS

Before you move forward, take time to sit with these questions:

1. What patterns in your life keep showing up, regardless of how you try to change them? That's Correspondence showing you a soul agreement still active.
2. Where does your life feel easy, like it's working with you instead of against you? That's alignment with what your Ori chose.
3. What doorway feels most natural for you to access this infinite field: meditation, prayer, dreams, divination, intuitive knowing?

PART II

CORRESPONDENCE

In Part I, we established the foundations. You learned that Egbe is your soul group that remembers you even when you've forgotten it. You met your Enikeji Orun, the eternal soul self that carries your essence across lifetimes. And you discovered the Universal Field, the infinite space where all consciousness converges, where Egbe and Enikeji Orun and everything else exists simultaneously.

Now you understand the cosmology. You know the players. You know where this all takes place.

Part II is where we move from concept to correspondence, from understanding what exists in Orun to recognizing how it shows up in Aiye. This is where the Law of Correspondence becomes practical: as above, so below. As within, so without. What your Ori agreed to in the spiritual realm is actively expressing itself in your physical life right now.

In the next three chapters, you'll learn what those agreements actually are, how your Egbe orchestrates circumstances to help you live them, and how your soul group fits within the larger constellation of spiritual relationships available to you.

This isn't abstract theology anymore. This is your life, explained.

Let's go.

THE AGREEMENTS YOUR ORI MADE: SOUL CONTRACTS THROUGH THE EGBE LENS

Understanding Ori: The Seat of Your Consciousness

Before we go deeper into what your Ori agreed to, we need to understand what Ori actually is.

In Yoruba cosmology, Ori (literally "head") is considered one of the most important divinities in the entire spiritual framework. It's not just your physical head. It's the seat of your consciousness, your destiny, and your inner self.

Ori has two aspects:

Ori Ode (the outer head) is your physical head. This is what people see when they look at you.

Ori Inu (the inner head) is your spiritual head. This is the part of you that holds your unique spiritual essence, your potential, your choices, and your connection to the divine. This is the aspect of Ori we're talking about when we discuss destiny and pre-birth agreements.

Here's what's important to understand: Ori is not something external to you. Ori is not a separate entity making decisions for you or blocking your path. Ori is you, the part of you that exists at soul frequency.

Think of it this way:

When you incarnated into this physical body, you didn't bring your entire consciousness with you. Part of you stayed in the spiritual realm as your Enikeji Orun. Part of you descended into physical form as your human personality. And the bridge between those two aspects, the part that holds your destiny blueprint and operates as your inner divinity, is your Ori Inu.

Your Ori chose your parents, your life circumstances, your challenges, your gifts, and your purpose before you were born. But once you're here, living this life, you don't experience Ori as something separate from you. You experience it as alignment or misalignment with what you already chose at the soul level.

When people say "your Ori approves" or "your Ori blocks" something, they're not talking about an external force granting permission. They're talking about vibrational congruence. When you're trying to do something that matches what your Ori chose, life tends to flow. When you're trying to force something that doesn't match your soul's blueprint, you feel friction. Not because Ori is punishing you, but because you're out of alignment with your own frequency.

This is "as above, so below" in action:

Above (Orun/spiritual realm): Your Ori exists as your destiny consciousness, holding the blueprint of what you came here to do.

Below (Aiye/physical realm): You exist as the incarnated expression, living out that blueprint.

Correspondence: When you're aligned with your Ori, you're vibrating at the same frequency as your destiny. You're not asking permission. You're remembering and embodying what you already chose.

In Yoruba thought, Ori is considered a personal deity. It's the most intimate aspect of your spiritual self, the part of you that mediates between you and all other spiritual forces. No other Orisa can override your Ori. Your ancestors cannot override your Ori. Your Egbe cannot override your Ori. It can support you, guide you, and orchestrate circumstances, but ultimately, what your Ori chose is what your life is meant to reflect.

The work, then, is not about pleading with Ori or trying to change what Ori chose. The work is about aligning your human consciousness with your Ori consciousness. This includes clearing the blocks, healing the wounds, releasing the conditioning, and remembering what you already agreed to before you were born.

When your Ori Inu is clear, when your inner head is in harmony with your soul's blueprint, life reflects that harmony. You experience *iwa-pele* (balanced character, good fortune, ease).

When your Ori Inu is clouded by trauma, conditioning, fear, or resistance, life feels hard. Not because Ori is withholding blessings, but because you're out of sync with your own frequency.

Keep this in mind as we move forward: Your Ori is the part of you that already knows why you're here. The question is whether you're listening.

The Agreements Your Ori Made

You've probably heard about "soul agreements" (the agreements made before birth about who you'd meet, what you'd learn, what you would experience).

You didn't come here by accident.

Before you were born, before you took your first breath, before you even had a name, your Ori made a choice. In that moment before incarnation, you selected the destiny you would carry into this lifetime.

You chose your parents. You chose your lessons. You chose the challenges that would shape you and the gifts that would define you. You chose the relationships that would break you open and the work that would call you forward. You chose the lifespan, the body, the circumstances that would become the container for your soul's expression in Aiye.

And your Egbe saw all of it.

Egbe: The Ones Who Observed and Agreed to Support

Your Egbe did not choose your destiny. It witnessed it.

In his book, Ayo Salami explains: "Enikeji Orun is entirely different from destiny (Ori). Enikeji Orun is strictly concerned with behaviors, not destiny" (*Egbe: The Heavenly Mates of Every Human*).

Your Enikeji Orun does not decide what your destiny will be. That is the work of Ori. Enikeji Orun is concerned with how you show up inside that destiny. It reflects, records, and responds to your choices and behaviors as you move through what Ori has chosen. Your Egbe participates in that witnessing field. It witnesses what your Ori selected and then orchestrates circumstances, relationships, and turning points that help you live those soul agreements in the most authentic way possible.

While your Ori was selecting your destiny and choosing your path, your Egbe was there watching. It heard the agreements you spoke. It understood what you were choosing to experience, what lessons you wanted to learn, what gifts you intended to bring, what relationships you would encounter, and what challenges you would face.

And here's the critical part: based on what it saw you choose, some members of your Egbe agreed to participate.

They said yes to being part of your journey. Not because they were assigned to you or obligated, but because they recognized how they could support what your Ori had chosen.

Maybe they agreed to incarnate alongside you as a family member, a friend, a teacher, a lover. Maybe they agreed to remain in Orun and orchestrate synchronicities from the spiritual realm. Maybe they agreed to hold the frequency of your purpose when you inevitably forgot it in the density of physical life.

Your Egbe is not a passive observer. It is an active participant in helping you live out what your Ori agreed to experience before you took your first breath.

So What Does This Actually Look Like?

Let me break down what those agreements are. Your agreements fall into several broad categories:

Relationship Agreements

Your Ori chose many of the souls you'd meet in this lifetime. Not every person you encounter is part of an agreement, but the ones who fundamentally shift you, the people who challenge you, teach you, break you open, or reflect your truth back to you, those are agreements.

Some relationship agreements are about growth through friction. You and another soul agreed to trigger each other's wounds so both of you could heal. These relationships often feel karmic, intense, and difficult to leave even when they're clearly not serving you. Soul-level work is happening beneath the surface drama.

Other relationship agreements are about support. These are the people who show up at exactly the right time with exactly what you need. The friend who believes in you when you don't believe in yourself. The mentor who sees your gifts before you do. The partner who holds space for your evolution. You agreed to meet them, and they agreed to support what you came here to do.

Some souls agreed to incarnate with you multiple times across different lifetimes, playing different roles. Your mother in this life might have been your child in another. Your closest friend might have been your sibling, your lover, or your teacher. These are deep soul bonds that transcend any single incarnation.

Gift Agreements

Before you were born, your Ori chose specific gifts for you to bring into this lifetime. Ori selected the talents, skills, and gifts that you would need to fulfill the destiny you chose.

If you are a natural healer, that is not an accident. Your Ori chose that gift before birth. If you are drawn to creative expression, teaching, organizing systems, working with your hands, or understanding complex information, whatever comes easily to you is part of your design.

Your gifts are not just for you. They are for the people you are meant to serve, the work you are meant to do, the contribution you are here to make. When you suppress your gifts or refuse to use them because you are scared, under-resourced, or convinced you are not good enough, you are violating your agreement. And your Egbe will create circumstances to push you back toward using what you came here to bring.

Lesson Agreements

You also chose specific lessons to learn in this lifetime. These are the recurring themes that show up across multiple relationships, situations, and life phases.

Maybe your lesson is about boundaries, learning to say no, to protect your energy, to stop giving yourself away. Maybe it is about trust, learning to rely on something larger than yourself. Maybe it is about self-worth, forgiveness, surrender, courage, or vulnerability.

Whatever your core lesson is, it will keep showing up in different forms until you learn it. Different people, different contexts, same core teaching. That is not bad luck. That is *Akunlegba*, the divine logistics system, creating the conditions for you to learn what you agreed to learn.

Challenge Agreements

This is the hardest part to sit with, so let me be direct about what I mean and what I do not mean.

When your Ori went to the house of Àjàlá to select your head, the challenges that you would face were also a part of that selection. Those challenges were not selected as punishment. They are not a result of you being tested by some external force, but because your soul knew that certain difficulties would catalyze specific growth.

If you have experienced loss, betrayal, illness, financial struggle, rejection, or any other form of hardship, it is possible that aspects of those experiences are tied to what your Ori selected as teachers. Not because you deserved them, but because you had the courage to say yes to particular forms of evolution as part of your soul's journey.

This does not mean you caused your trauma. It does not mean you should bypass healing or accept mistreatment. It means that even in your hardest moments, there is a larger context at play, a soul-level agreement that can give your suffering meaning beyond the pain itself.

When I say your Ori chose your challenges, I am not saying you caused your trauma or deserved your pain. Some Ori choose to experience profound difficulty, including specific lessons or contributions to collective healing that require walking through fire.

But your Ori choosing a challenge before birth does not mean you waive your right to heal from it. It does not mean you are supposed to stay in abusive situations. It does not mean the perpetrator is off the hook because "it was your agreement."

These types of agreements explain the spiritual context. They do not excuse harm or bypass accountability.

If you have experienced trauma, you need healing. You need support. You need to process what happened in safe, grounded ways. The spiritual framework does not replace therapy, medical care, or practical action.

What soul agreements do offer is a larger perspective. They help you see that your suffering is not random, that you are not being punished, and that there is a purpose larger than the pain itself. That perspective can be deeply healing, but it is not a substitute for the actual work of healing.

Déjà Vu as Soul Agreement Confirmation

For years, I struggled with déjà vu. That eerie feeling of "I've been here before" when you know you haven't. That sense of living through something that feels like a memory but can't possibly be one.

I tried all the conventional explanations. Brain glitches. Parallel dimensions. Past lives bleeding through. But none of them felt right for my experience.

Now I understand what déjà vu actually is, at least for me: confirmation from my Egbe that I'm hitting the set points I agreed to before I was born.

Let me explain what I mean by set points.

Before you descended into Aiye, we have already established that you chose your destiny. However, not everything was planned down to the minute. Most of your path is fluid. There are multiple ways to get where you are going, multiple people who could play certain roles, multiple timelines that could work.

But some things? Some things are non-negotiable. These are what I call set points.

Before I left Orun, I might have agreed: "On January 15th at 3 PM, I'm going to be at this gathering with these particular souls." Those other souls, part of my Egbe, made the same agreement. We committed to showing up at that specific moment, in that specific configuration, for reasons our human selves might not even understand.

How we get there? That's fluid. I might take three different jobs before landing in the city where that gathering happens. I might meet the host through a chance encounter, or a mutual friend, or a random invitation I almost decline. The path to the set point can vary wildly.

But the set point itself? Non-negotiable.

When I arrive at that gathering, when I look around and see those faces, when the moment crystallizes exactly as it was meant to, that is when déjà vu hits.

It's not my brain malfunctioning. It's my soul recognizing: "Yes. This is one of our set points. We made it to where we agreed to be."

For me, déjà vu has become confirmation from my Egbe that I'm on task. That despite all the twists and turns, all the apparent detours, all the times I thought I was lost, I'm actually exactly where I'm supposed to be, when I'm supposed to be there.

It's not about the intermediary things. It's not about whether I took the scenic route or got there early or arrived at the last minute. It's about recognition: "We agreed to this moment before you were born, and here we are. You honored the agreement."

That's Egbe support in action. That's how it confirms alignment without having to send dramatic signs or speak in booming voices from the sky. It arranged for you to experience the moment exactly as planned, and your soul's recognition of that arrangement is what creates the déjà vu sensation.

Now when I feel that familiar flutter, that sense of "this has all happened before," I don't dismiss it or try to explain it away. I pay attention. I look around. I ask: "What's significant about this moment? Who am I with? What's happening that my soul pre-arranged?"

Because if I'm experiencing déjà vu, it means I've hit a set point. And if I've hit a set point, it means I'm aligned with my agreements, my Egbe is orchestrating successfully, and whatever's about to unfold was planned before I took my first breath.

That's not fate, that's collaboration between your human choices and your soul's wisdom, playing out exactly as designed.

You might have experienced this as:

- Walking into a new place as glimpses of it surfaces in your mind
- A conversation that feels like you've had it before, word for word

That recognition? That's your soul remembering the set points you agreed to. That's your Egbe confirming you're on path.

When Soul Agreements Create Earthly Challenges

Let me tell you about a client who came to me desperate for answers.

She was in her thirties. She'd been dating for over a decade, actively, intentionally trying to build a lasting relationship. And every single time, the same pattern would unfold. Things would start beautifully. Connection, chemistry, potential. She'd think, "This is it. This is finally the one."

And then, out of nowhere, it would end. Abruptly. Sometimes the man would ghost. Sometimes he'd give a reason that made no sense. Sometimes she'd be the one who suddenly felt the need to leave, even though nothing was actually wrong.

Ten years of this. Dozens of relationships. The same inexplicable pattern.

When she came to work with me, we opened her Akashic Records first. That's where I saw it: a soul mate contract. An agreement made before this lifetime about partnership and love. But there was something else underneath it, something the Records were pointing to but not fully revealing.

I was guided to tell her she needed a consultation with Egbe.

During the Egbe divination, the truth came through clearly: she had a husband in Orun. And that relationship in Orun was blocking her ability to have a successful love life here in Aiye.

She looked at me confused. "A husband in Orun? What does that even mean? Why would I agree to that if I wanted to be in a relationship here?"

Here's what I explained to her: Some souls make agreements that span both Orun and Aiye. Her eternal soul self had a mate in the spiritual realm. That wasn't a punishment. It was an agreement. And part of that agreement for THIS lifetime was about learning sovereignty and independence, not partnership.

The pattern wasn't a failure. It was Egbe honoring what her Ori chose before birth.

We did a traditional Isese ceremony to separate the *Oko* (husband) in Orun. The ceremony acknowledged the spiritual relationship while creating space for her to have an earthly one if she chose.

Within months, the pattern shifted. She met someone. The relationship unfolded naturally. No abrupt endings. No inexplicable resistance.

Understanding the agreement didn't mean fighting it. It meant honoring what her soul had chosen and then making a conscious choice about whether she wanted to continue that agreement or release it.

A Single Closing Reflection

You've now seen the difference between what your Ori chose, what external forces conditioned you to want, and what your wounds made you believe you needed. Three different things. And the soul agreements you made before birth are woven through all of it.

You now have a clearer sense of what your Ori agreed to. The next question is this: How does your Egbe actually bring those agreements to life in real time?

REFLECTION QUESTIONS

Before you move forward, take time to sit with these questions:

1. What pattern in your life keeps showing up regardless of circumstances? Different relationships, different jobs, different cities, but the same core lesson.
2. What have you been blaming on bad luck or external circumstances that might actually be a soul-level agreement?
3. If you knew with certainty that you chose your current challenges before birth, how would that change your relationship to them?

CHAPTER 5

HOW THE UNSEEN INFLUENCES THE SEEN: EGBE ORCHESTRATING YOUR LIFE

You know WHAT your Ori agreed to: the relationships, gifts, challenges, lessons. Now let's talk about HOW those agreements actually show up in your daily life.

Your Egbe doesn't simply remember what your Ori chose. It actively works from Orun to shape your experience in Aiye: arranging meetings, creating opportunities, and yes, sometimes dismantling entire structures to redirect you when you've wandered off the path your Ori laid out.

What exists in Orun doesn't just influence Aiye. It orchestrates it. As above, so below. What your Egbe holds in the unseen shapes what unfolds in the seen. Your life isn't random. It's not chaos punctuated by occasional meaning. It's the continuous expression of what your soul agreed to, guided by the hands of those who saw that agreement.

Orun and Aiye aren't separate realms. They're interconnected, constantly influencing each other. Most people don't realize how active this influence is until they look back and see the patterns. The job that ended right before you found your calling. The relationship that dissolved just in time for you to meet someone aligned with your truth. The illness that forced you to stop and reassess everything.

That's not luck. That's Egbe at work. Here's how this played out in my own life.

How Egbe's Orchestration Showed Up in My Life

I mentioned in Chapter 1 how the taboo against lying I received during initiation unraveled everything. Let me show you how that orchestration continued.

Dishonesty had always felt wrong to me, so receiving a taboo against something I already didn't do felt almost unnecessary. But I sat with it anyway. And the profundity of that simple statement, "do not tell a lie," continued to dismantle all the ways I had been performing life.

Once I saw it, I couldn't unsee it.

My soul had given me the taboo to wake me up. And now that I was awake, my Egbe started showing me all the ways this lie was woven through my life: every choice I had made to please others, every time I had ignored my intuition, every moment I had chosen safety over truth.

I made the difficult decision to separate from my marriage. I'm not advocating that separation or divorce is the answer for everyone, but for me, it was the first major step in honoring what my soul had been trying to tell me for years.

During that separation process, while my external life was falling apart, something unexpected happened: I discovered the Akashic Records.

I started learning about this metaphysical concept, an infinite field where all soul-level information is stored. I began studying the soul self, soul agreements, pre-birth choices. All of this information was flowing to me precisely because I'd made the choice to follow what had come from my Egbe, because I was willing to stop lying to myself and start living truthfully.

It felt like my Egbe had opened a door. The moment I honored the taboo by choosing authenticity, it orchestrated my access to deeper spiritual knowledge that would become the foundation of my life's work.

I started practicing with the Akashic Records, initially just for myself and close friends. I wasn't trying to build a business. I was simply following what felt alive, what felt true. And the more I followed that pull, the more I realized I was in complete flow.

Every time I took a step forward, the universe responded. Opportunities appeared without me looking for them. The right people showed up at exactly the right time. Resources materialized. I was living in a state of synchronicity so constant it stopped feeling like coincidence and started feeling like collaboration.

At the end of my second year doing Akashic Records readings professionally, I realized I had made as much money doing this spiritual work as I was making in my current salaried job. It hit me with absolute clarity: this is alignment.

This was what my Ori had chosen. This was what my Egbe had been trying to guide me toward all along: the path of spiritual work, of teaching, of helping people understand where they are living in societal conditioning versus soul truth. I just had to be willing to live in the unconventional and truly follow what my spirit had been telling me all along.

That taboo against lying became the key that unlocked everything. My Egbe used it to show me where I was out of alignment. And when I corrected that misalignment, it orchestrated the circumstances that led me directly to my purpose.

That's how Egbe works. It creates the conditions, sometimes through gifts, sometimes through disruption, that pull you back to the path your Ori chose.

When Life Flows: Signs You're Aligned

When you're living in alignment with your choices, life has a particular quality to it.

Synchronicity becomes normal. Things click into place. Doors open easily. The right people appear at the right time. Resources show up when you need them. You think of something and it manifests faster than expected. This is what happens when the unseen and seen are working together, when your Egbe can move freely to support what you're already aligned with.

Your gifts flow naturally. The work doesn't feel forced. Your creativity, intuition, capacity to heal, teach, lead, or create feels like it's coming through you, not from you. Because it is. These gifts are agreements your Ori made, witnessed by your Egbe, and they flow most powerfully when you're on your chosen path.

You feel supported, even in difficulty. Alignment doesn't mean life is easy. It means even when things are hard, you have a sense of purpose. You feel like you're growing through it. Your Egbe doesn't remove all challenges. Some are part of what you agreed to. But when you're aligned, you feel held through difficulty. You feel guided.

Clarity replaces confusion. Decisions feel simpler. You know what's yours and what's not. You can discern between what your soul chose and what conditioning imposed. That clarity is Egbe speaking through your intuition, affirming what you already know at a soul level.

People and opportunities arrive without force. You stop chasing. You stop hustling to make things happen. Instead, you move in the direction your soul is pulling you, and life meets you there. Collaborations form. Teachers appear. The community you need finds you.

When you're aligned, life doesn't feel like a battle. It feels like a dance. You're still moving, still working, still showing up, but you're in rhythm with something larger than yourself.

When Life Disrupts: Signs You're Off-Path

When you've forgotten what you came here to do, when you're living someone else's expectations, when you're ignoring your agreements, your Egbe intervenes.

Repeated loss or failure in specific areas. If every job in a particular field falls through, if every relationship follows the same dysfunctional pattern, if money keeps slipping away no matter how hard you work, that's not bad luck. That's Egbe creating friction. It's not blocking you to be cruel. It's blocking you because that path isn't aligned with what you agreed to.

Physical and emotional exhaustion. When you're living out of alignment, your body knows before your mind does. You get sick. You burn out. You feel depleted no matter how much rest you get. You're using energy to maintain something that doesn't serve your soul. Your Egbe is pulling that energy away to force you to stop, reassess, and realign.

Persistent dissatisfaction despite external success. You have everything you thought you wanted, but something feels hollow. You keep waiting to feel fulfilled and it never comes. That's Egbe whispering that this isn't what you chose. And no amount of external achievement will fill the void of soul-level misalignment.

Dreams that feel like warnings. You dream of being lost, missing flights, being unprepared. You dream of water rising, babies crying, unfamiliar people calling your name. These aren't nightmares. They're communications. Your Egbe is trying to get your attention through the channel that bypasses your waking resistance.

Things falling apart in rapid succession. When multiple structures collapse at once, it's not random. Your Egbe is dismantling what wasn't aligned so you can rebuild on the foundation of what you actually chose.

This is where people panic. They think they're cursed, that something is wrong with them, that they're being punished. But that's not what's happening. Your Egbe is protecting you from wasting your life on paths you never chose, identities you never selected.

The disruption is an act of love. It's your soul group in Orun saying, "Remember. Come back. This isn't what you came here for."

How to Work With Egbe Consciously

Here's how to actively collaborate with your Egbe instead of unconsciously resisting them:

Notice the patterns

Where does life keep pushing you? Where do doors keep closing despite your efforts? Where do doors keep opening even when you're uncertain? Those patterns are Egbe showing you where you're aligned and where you're not.

Practice: Keep a synchronicity journal. When something feels "too perfect to be coincidence," write it down. Note the date, the circumstance, what happened. Over time, you'll see Egbe's signature style of orchestration. You'll start recognizing its hand before the full pattern unfolds.

Trust your body

Your Egbe speaks through discomfort, through longing, through the places where you feel alive and the places where you feel dead inside. Your body knows the truth before your mind catches up. Trust it.

Practice: Use the "pause and check" technique. When you feel resistance, stop and ask: "Is this fear speaking, or is this my Egbe showing me I'm off-path?" Fear feels constricting, tight, based in old wounds. Egbe's redirection feels clarifying, even when uncomfortable. It opens something rather than closing it.

Pay attention to dreams

Dreams are one of the primary ways Egbe communicates in Yoruba tradition. Pay attention to recurring images: water, gatherings, children, dancing, unfamiliar places that feel like home. These aren't random. They're messages.

Practice: Keep a dream journal by your bed. Before sleep, ask: "What do I need to know?" Write down what you remember immediately upon waking, even fragments. Look for patterns over time.

How to recognize Egbe dreams vs. processing dreams:

- **Egbe dreams** feel urgent, vivid, emotionally charged. You wake up knowing something important happened. They often involve gatherings, being called, water, dancing, or people you don't know but feel you should.
- **Processing dreams** feel more chaotic, fragmented, directly tied to recent events or anxieties. They're your mind sorting through the day's experiences.

Both matter, but Egbe dreams carry information meant to guide you.

Create stillness

Egbe can't guide you if you're too busy to hear them. Meditation, prayer, nature, silence—these aren't luxuries. They're how you create conditions for Egbe to speak and for you to listen.

Practice: Even five minutes of silence daily creates space for Egbe to communicate. You don't need elaborate ritual. Consistent presence works. Sit quietly. Breathe. Place your hand on your head (the seat of Ori) and connect with the earth beneath you. Ask: "What are you trying to show me?" Then listen without expectation.

Align your actions

Once you recognize what you came here to do, do it. Use your gifts. Follow the pull. Make the changes that terrify you but feel true at a soul level. The more aligned your actions, the more your Egbe can support you. The more flow you experience.

Practice: Ask yourself daily: "Is what I'm doing today honoring what I came here to do?" This one question keeps you in dialogue with your Egbe. You don't need a perfect answer. Just the practice of asking creates alignment.

Ask them directly

If you're confused, stuck, unsure what your Egbe wants from you—ask them. Out loud. In prayer. In meditation. In your journal.

"What did my Ori agree to? Where am I off-path? What needs my attention?"

Then pay attention to what shows up: a conversation, a synchronicity, a dream, a sudden knowing. It will answer. It always does.

Your Egbe doesn't just witness your agreements. It actively creates the conditions that allow those agreements to manifest in Aiye. The synchronicities, the disruptions, the dreams, the patterns—none of it's random. It's the unseen influencing the seen, Orun shaping Aiye, your soul group in heaven guiding your life on earth.

When you learn to recognize it's hand in your life, when you stop resisting and start collaborating, everything changes.

But your Egbe isn't the only spiritual force supporting your journey.

REFLECTION QUESTIONS

Before you move forward, take time to sit with these questions:

1. Look back at a moment when life fell apart but led to something better. Can you see your Egbe's hand in that now?
2. Where are you currently forcing something that keeps meeting resistance? What would happen if you stopped pushing?
3. What would your life look like if you trusted that every door that closes is your Egbe redirecting you toward what your Ori actually chose?

CHAPTER 6

MULTIPLE SPIRITUAL RELATIONSHIPS: EGBE, ANCESTORS, ORISA, GUIDES, UNIVERSAL FORCES

Here's a question I get constantly: 'If I work with my Egbe, do I still work with my ancestors? What about my spirit guides? Where do the Orisa fit in? Am I supposed to choose?'

No. You don't choose. You have multiple spiritual relationships happening simultaneously, and they're all part of the same ecosystem. Let me show you how.

Your Egbe is not replacing your ancestors or guides. Each serves a different function. Your Egbe isn't the only force supporting your evolution. You're part of a web of spiritual kinship that includes your lineage, universal forces, and consciousness itself.

This chapter is about understanding who's who in your spiritual ecosystem, what role each plays, and how to discern whose voice is whose. Because when you understand the different players and their functions, you stop feeling confused and start feeling supported by the network of consciousness that's been holding you all along.

A Note on Scope: The Spiritual Forces in This Book

The spiritual relationships I focus on in this chapter (Ori, Enikeji Orun, Egbe, Orisa, ancestors, and guides) aren't the only spiritual forces that exist.

Depending on your background, you may also work with angels, archangels, ascended masters, deities from other traditions, saints, bodhisattvas, or other spiritual beings. I honor those relationships, and I'm not suggesting you set them aside.

I also want to acknowledge that some of the forces I teach (particularly spirit guides) don't come directly from mainland Isese cosmology. Spirit guides are a diasporic adaptation that emerged through practices like Espiritismo in Cuba and have since become integral to how many of us in the Americas work with spiritual support. I include them here because they are a vital part of my work, my teaching, and the lived experience of African diaspora practitioners.

My focus here is on the forces most common in my work with clients and how your soul agreements show up in your life. If you work with other spiritual beings, you can absolutely integrate them into this framework. The principles of correspondence, alignment, and soul-level agreements apply universally, no matter what tradition or language you're using.

Mapping Your Spiritual Support System

Think of your spiritual relationships as a web with you at the center.

At the center is you, not your human personality, but your Enikeji Orun. The you that's both individual and inseparable from Universal Consciousness.

Closest to you is your Egbe. It saw your pre-birth agreements and actively works to keep you aligned with what your Ori chose.

Beyond Egbe are your ancestors, the spirits of your bloodline who carry accumulated wisdom, trauma, gifts, and patterns of your lineage.

Then there are spirit guides, teachers and helpers who are assigned or chosen to support your specific soul journey in this lifetime.

The Orisa exist as universal forces, principles of nature and consciousness that anyone can align with regardless of personal relationships.

And holding all of this is Source, Universal Consciousness, Olodumare, the infinite field from which everything emerges and to which everything returns. Not separate from you, but the essence of what you are.

Who's Who: Roles and Functions

Let me break down what each force actually does.

Ori: Your Inner Consciousness and Destiny Selector

Ori is your inner head, your personal divinity, the aspect of you that chose your destiny before birth. Ori went to Àjàlá's house and selected the head that would hold your potential, your gifts, your challenges, and your purpose for this lifetime.

Ori is the deepest part of your consciousness in this incarnation. When you honor your Ori, you're honoring the choices your soul made before you forgot them.

Enikeji Orun: Your Eternal Soul Self

Enikeji Orun is your heavenly double, the eternal aspect of you that exists in Orun while you navigate Aiye. This isn't a separate being watching you from a distance. This is you, the version that didn't drink from *omi igbagbe* (the river of forgetfulness), the part that remembers what your human self forgot.

Your Enikeji Orun doesn't choose your destiny (that's Ori's job), but it holds the pattern of who you are across all lifetimes, carrying forward what hasn't been resolved, learned, or expressed.

Egbe: Your Soul Group and Orchestrators

Egbe is your spiritual collective, the group of souls you belong to across lifetimes. It witnessed what your Ori chose before birth and agreed to support you in living those agreements. It doesn't just remember. It actively orchestrates circumstances, synchronicities, and disruptions to keep you aligned with your path.

Egbe creates the set points in your life: the people you were meant to meet, the opportunities that appear at exactly the right time, the doors that won't open no matter how hard you push because that direction isn't what you agreed to.

It's not managing your life from some distant heaven. It IS you, the collective aspect of you, holding the frequency of your purpose while your human self navigates density.

Ifa: The Library of Destinies

Ifa (often spoken of together with Orunmila, the Orisa of wisdom and destiny) is both a divination system and a body of wisdom that contains all human experiences and lessons. Ifa was present when every Ori chose its path before incarnation. Ifa is the record-keeper, the witness to all destinies, the holder of universal wisdom about how souls navigate Aiye. The system reveals what your Ori chose, what agreements are active, and what offerings or actions will support your alignment.

The core question Ifa divination answers is: *Am I in alignment with my destiny?*

Ifa doesn't create your destiny or change your agreements. It reveals them so you can work with them consciously.

Orisa: Universal Forces

The Orisa aren't personal guides. They're universal forces, expressions of nature and consciousness that govern aspects of existence. Oshun embodies love, beauty, fertility, and self-worth. Oya governs transformation, change, and the storm. Ogun represents work, technology, and clearing paths. Shango is fire, justice, and power.

These aren't beings who know you personally or care about your individual journey the way Egbe does. They're principles. When you align with an Orisa's energy, you're aligning with a frequency, a force that's always available but doesn't seek you out.

You can call on Orisa energy when you need to embody a particular principle, but they don't orchestrate your life. That's Egbe's work.

Ancestors: Your Lineage Connection

Your ancestors are the spirits of your bloodline, those who came before you, whose DNA you carry, whose stories shaped the family you were born into. They carry accumulated wisdom from generations of lived experience. They also carry trauma, unresolved patterns, and wounds that get passed down until someone in the lineage heals them.

Working with ancestors means:

- Acknowledging the sacrifices they made so you could be here
- Honoring the gifts they passed down: resilience, creativity, spiritual capacity

- Healing the patterns that no longer serve: addiction, abuse, limitation, fear
- Carrying forward the wisdom while releasing the wounds

Your ancestors are invested in your wellbeing because your success is their success. When you heal, you heal the lineage backward and forward. When you thrive, you fulfill dreams they couldn't complete.

But ancestors are not the same as Egbe. Ancestors are bound by blood. Egbe are bound by soul agreements that transcend bloodlines and lifetimes.

Spirit Guides: Teachers and Perspective Holders

Spirit guides are teachers, helpers, and perspective holders who work with you for specific periods or lessons. They're not emotionally invested in your choices the way Egbe is. They don't carry your lineage patterns the way ancestors do. They offer neutral wisdom, practical insight, and teaching.

Some guides stay with you for your entire life. Others come for a season, teach what they came to teach, and move on. They help you see blind spots, offer alternative perspectives, and support you in developing specific skills or understanding.

Guides don't orchestrate your life. But they illuminate the path Egbe is creating so you can navigate it more consciously.

Source: Universal Consciousness

Source is the infinite field, the consciousness from which everything emerges and to which everything returns. It's not a being with preferences or personality. It's the essence underlying all existence.

Source isn't something you work with; it's what you are. Your Enikeji Orun, your Egbe, the Orisa, your ancestors, all of it exists within Source. And so do you.

When you return to Source through stillness, meditation, or prayer, you're not reaching out to something external. You're remembering what you've always been part of.

How to Discern Who's Speaking

When you open yourself to spiritual guidance, multiple voices become available. Learning to discern who's speaking and what they're offering is essential.

Egbe feels like resonance and recognition. It's the pull toward something you can't explain but know is yours. It's the synchronicity that makes you laugh because it's so obvious. It's the disruption that feels devastating but leads somewhere better. Egbe's voice is both familiar and insistent because it's holding the memory of what you agreed to.

Ancestors feel like inheritance. It's the pattern you recognize from your family line, the strength you didn't know you had until you needed it, the wound that keeps showing up until you heal it. Ancestors speak through your body, your emotional triggers, your inexplicable knowing about how to survive.

Guides feel like teaching. It's the insight that arrives when you're stuck, the perspective you couldn't see on your own, the practical wisdom that helps you navigate complexity. Guides don't have emotional charge. Their voice is clear, neutral, supportive.

Orisa feel like force. It's not personal like Egbe. It's universal, powerful, often transformative. Orisa energy changes you by aligning you with principles larger than your individual journey.

Source feels like remembering. It doesn't feel like receiving information from outside yourself. It feels like recognizing something you've always known. It's the quietest voice and the loudest truth, the space where all other voices dissolve into one.

The more you practice discernment, the easier it becomes to recognize who's speaking and what they're offering.

When Everything Shifts at Once: A Complete Example

Let me show you how all these forces work together.

Meet Summer. She's 38, stuck in a marketing job that pays well but drains her soul. She's been having vivid dreams of teaching and speaking. Her marriage feels more like a business partnership than a love connection. Her body is sending signals: chronic migraines, insomnia, digestive issues that won't resolve.

She keeps telling herself to be grateful. She has stability, health insurance, a nice home. But the discomfort is growing unbearable.

Here's what's actually happening in her spiritual ecosystem:

Ori chose this lifetime to learn about creative expression, spiritual teaching, and aligned partnership. Before birth, Ori selected the lessons that would require her to leave behind security and step into the unknown.

Egbe witnessed what Ori chose and orchestrates circumstances to keep Summer aligned. It arranged for her to take the corporate job first because learning what drains you is part of learning what fulfills you. It's sending dreams of teaching as reminders. It's creating health issues because misalignment shows up in the body first.

Enikeji Orun remains in Orun holding the fullness of who she is: the teacher, the creator, the spiritually activated woman who came here to help others remember their soul agreements.

Ifa (when Summer finally consults a diviner) reveals she has *ori ibi*, a confused head. The divination confirms this job isn't aligned with her path, this marriage lacks the spiritual depth her Ori chose to experience, and her health issues are spiritual misalignment manifesting physically. Ifa prescribes offerings to Oshun for self-love, Oya for courage in transition, and to her Egbe to reestablish conscious connection.

Oya's energy becomes available when Summer begins considering leaving the job. Oya governs transformation and the courage to walk through the storm. Summer aligns with this universal force, and it supports her capacity to move through change without falling apart.

Oshun's energy supports Summer in recognizing her worth beyond what she produces. When she considers that she deserves love that sees her fully, she's aligning with Oshun's frequency of self-love and worthiness.

Summer's ancestors show up in three ways: Her maternal grandmother was an artist who gave up painting when she married and resented it for forty years. That pattern lives in Summer's DNA—the choice between creative fulfillment and security. Her paternal lineage carries patterns of staying silent and not making waves, which is why leaving feels so terrifying. Her great-aunt left an abusive marriage in the 1950s and built a life alone. That strength lives in Summer too, passed down through the lineage.

Spirit guides offer practical perspective in meditation: You're not choosing between security and risk. You're choosing between slow death and alignment. The risk is staying where you are. They teach her how to discern her truth from fear-based thinking.

Source, the infinite field underneath everything, says: *You are not separate from any of this. You are me experiencing myself through this particular configuration of consciousness. The job doesn't define you. The marriage doesn't define you. You are the eternal awareness witnessing all of it. Trust the unfolding.*

What happens next: Summer gives notice at her job on a Thursday morning. By Friday afternoon, someone emails asking if she's available to lead a workshop. Within a week, two more opportunities appear. This isn't coincidence. This is Egbe orchestrating what it's been preparing for years.

The marriage ends more slowly, through honest conversations and grief. Within a year of the separation, Summer meets someone who understands her spiritual depth, not because she "manifested" him, but because Egbe orchestrated their paths crossing at the exact moment both were ready.

Her health issues resolve within three months of leaving the job. The migraines disappear. Sleep returns. Her body stops screaming because she finally listened.

The takeaway? Every force in Summer's spiritual ecosystem was working together, each playing its role: Ori chose the lessons. Egbe orchestrated the circumstances. Enikeji Orun held the eternal pattern. Ifa provided confirmation and guidance. Orisa offered universal principles. Ancestors passed down gifts and wounds to be healed. Guides taught discernment. Source reminded her she was never separate from any of it.

This is how the ecosystem works. Not in isolation. In collaboration. All forces moving together to support the soul's evolution, honoring the agreements made before birth, ensuring the lessons chosen in Orun get lived in Aiye.

Working With All of Them Without Losing Yourself

Here's the key: you don't have to choose.

Your spiritual relationships aren't competing for attention. They're all supporting you in different ways.

Honor your Egbe by living in alignment with your soul's agreements, using your gifts, allowing it to orchestrate your path.

Honor your ancestors by acknowledging the lineage you come from, healing what needs healing, carrying forward the wisdom they've passed down.

Work with guides when you need perspective, teaching, or insight that helps you navigate specific challenges.

Call on the Orisa when you need to align with universal principles (protection, love, transformation, wisdom) that support your work.

Return to Source regularly through stillness, prayer, or meditation to remember that all these relationships are expressions of the same consciousness you're part of.

And most importantly: trust your Enikeji Orun. You aren't separate from any of these forces. You are the living bridge between Orun and Aiye, the one carrying all these relationships into form.

Think of it this way: Orisa are the laws of nature. Egbe is your personal support team. Ifa is the library of destinies. Ori is your unique blueprint. Ancestors are your lineage. Source is the infinite field holding it all.

What exists above shows up below. Your Egbe, holding the memory of what your Ori chose, creates circumstances that reflect those choices. Your ancestors pass down patterns that shape how you move through the world. The Orisa embody universal principles that are also active within you. Source holds all of it (the individual and the collective, the personal and the universal) in one infinite field.

You don't have to understand it all perfectly. You just have to stay open, pay attention, and trust that when you need support, the right force will make itself known.

Honoring the Tradition

These teachings are rooted in Yoruba cosmology, but the principles are universal. Every tradition has some version of soul groups, destiny selection, and the eternal soul self. The Yoruba framework offers one cultural lens for understanding these universal truths.

You can work with these concepts without initiation. What you can't do is conduct Ifa divination without training or lead Egbe ceremonies without proper initiation. Know the difference.

The wisdom is universal. The ceremonial practices are tradition-specific. Honor both by being clear about what you're doing and who taught you. If you feel called to formal initiation, seek out legitimate teachers rooted in the tradition. If you're applying these principles to understand your own spiritual journey, you're doing exactly what this book is designed to help you do.

REFLECTION QUESTIONS

Before you move forward, take time to sit with these questions:

1. Which spiritual relationships do you already have conscious connection with? Which ones feel unfamiliar or distant?
2. When you sit in stillness, can you feel the difference between Egbe's resonance, ancestors' inheritance, guides' teaching, and Source's remembering?
3. Where in your life do you need Egbe's orchestration versus ancestors' healing versus guides' perspective? Can you discern what support you're actually asking for?
4. How would your relationship with spiritual support shift if you trusted that all these forces are working together, not competing for your attention?

PART III

ALIGNMENT & INTEGRATION

You've covered a lot of ground. By now you understand the structure of your soul (Ori, Egbe, Enikeji Orun) and how these aspects work together. You know what soul agreements are and how they were made. You've seen how Egbe orchestrates your life from behind the scenes, arranging the synchronicities and encounters that keep you on path. And you understand how your soul group relates to ancestors, Orisa, guides, and other spiritual forces.

Understanding the system is important. But understanding isn't the same as living it.

Part III is about embodiment. This is where we move from knowing to being, from concept to practice, from theory to the messy, beautiful reality of living soul-aligned in a physical body, in real time, with actual challenges.

In the next three chapters, you'll see what it looks like to live your agreements through personal narrative and practical guidance. You'll learn how to nurture your spiritual relationships without making them weird, performative, or dependent. And you'll discover what it means to be the bridge: not someone crossing between worlds, but the living connection between Orun and Aiye, embodying as above, so below in your daily existence.

This is where it gets real. This is where you stop reading about the work and start doing it.

CHAPTER 7

LIVING YOUR AGREEMENTS: WHEN EGBE WON'T LET YOU HIDE

Understanding your agreements intellectually is one thing. Living them is another.

There's a difference between knowing something spiritually and living it in your bones. None of the cosmology means anything until you're standing in the middle of your actual life (facing a choice that costs you something) and you feel your agreements pulling at you from the inside.

That's what this chapter is about: what it actually looks like to live your agreements when it gets uncomfortable.

The Taboo That Changed Everything

I shared the outline of this story in Chapter 1, but now I want to take you deeper into what it actually felt like to live it.

I had been unhappy for a while in my marriage. Not in the dramatic, explosive way that makes for good stories, but in that quiet, gnawing way where your spirit is screaming at you and you keep turning the volume down because you don't want to deal with what it's saying.

I had contemplated leaving my marriage many times before the initiation. But every time the thought came up, I would push it down. I'd tell myself all the reasons why staying made sense: What will people think? What does it mean if I can't make this work? What about the kids? What about being a "broken family"?

I was buying into societal programming about what marriage should look like, what failure looked like, what it meant to be a good partner, a good parent, a good person. And so I stayed. Even though everything in my spirit was telling me it was time to go.

But post-initiation, my Egbe wasn't letting me get away with it anymore.

The Lie I'd Been Living

The taboo about lying forced me to confront something I'd been avoiding for years: I was lying to myself.

Not about specific facts. Not in the way most people think about lying. I was lying about being happy when I wasn't. I was lying about being fulfilled when I was dying inside. I was lying about my marriage being something it wasn't, because I was too afraid to face what leaving would mean.

And now, with this Egbe taboo, the mismatch between what I was telling myself and what I was actually living became unbearable. Every day felt heavier. The dissonance was crushing. I couldn't pretend anymore that everything was fine when my soul was screaming that it wasn't.

That's when I realized: The lie my Egbe was calling out wasn't about deceiving someone else. It was about betraying myself. I was living according to societal programming (what society says a "good marriage" looks like, what a "broken family" means, what it says about you if you can't make it work) instead of living according to my soul's truth.

And my Egbe taboo was forcing me to confront that.

PROGRAMMING REALIZATION

Once I understood that the taboo against lying was really about lying to myself, everything shifted.

I started to see how much of what I'd been living wasn't actually mine. The marriage I was trying to save? That wasn't about love or partnership. That was about societal programming. About what I'd been taught a successful marriage should look like. About not creating a "broken family." About being a "good wife" who makes it work no matter what.

None of that was from my soul. It was conditioning.

And that realization opened up my entire life's work.

Because now, when I work with clients, one of the first things I help them identify is where they're operating from societal, ancestral, or karmic programming instead of their own soul's truth. This is the distinction I mentioned in Chapter 4, the difference between inherited beliefs and soul agreements.

Most people don't realize how much of what they're living is inherited. Beliefs about success, relationships, money, purpose. Scripts passed down from parents, culture, religion, media. Programs running in the background that were never theirs to begin with.

My Egbe taboo made it impossible to avoid seeing what I'd been hiding from myself. It made it impossible for me to keep living the lie.

Timeline Clarification

Let me be clear about how this unfolded:

2015 (July): Egbe initiation in Nigeria. Received the taboo against lying.

2016 (June): Separated from my spouse. Moved to Tallahassee to start my position at Florida State University. Got my first Akashic Records reading as a client.

2017: Started learning to read the Akashic Records myself.

2018: Started taking clients for Akashic Records readings.

2019: CHI Healing Institute officially became a business.

2025: Left my academic position.

Once I came back from Nigeria, the incongruence became impossible to live with. It wasn't gradual. It was rapid. I could no longer ignore the mismatch between what I was telling myself and what my soul knew to be true.

By June 2016, less than a year later, I had separated from my spouse. And that same month, I moved to Tallahassee to start a new position at Florida State University.

It was painful. It was messy. It required me to face judgments, both from others and from myself. But it was also the most honest thing I'd ever done. And once I stopped lying to myself, once I started living according to my agreements instead of society's expectations, the doors started opening.

What Came After

The period after leaving my marriage was rough. Two kids depending on me. New job that I was still figuring out. Completely different financial situation: from stability to uncertainty, from a life that looked good on paper to building a life that felt good in real time.

But here's what I learned, what I know now with absolute certainty: when you follow the breadcrumbs, even when it costs you comfort, safety, what you know, they lead you home.

Every synchronicity I followed (the class that appeared at exactly the right time, the mentor who reached out unexpectedly, the download that came through at 3am that I actually listened to instead of dismissing) was a breadcrumb. Egbe orchestrating the path forward because I'd finally stopped lying to myself and to it about what I was really here to do.

That taboo wasn't about small deceptions or social niceties. It was about the fundamental dishonesty of living a life that looked right while knowing it was wrong. The dishonesty of staying in a marriage that was killing my soul because leaving seemed too hard. The dishonesty of playing small because claiming my actual calling seemed too risky.

When I honored that taboo, when I finally told the truth even though it cost me my marriage, my financial security, my sense of stability, everything shifted.

Not immediately. The shift wasn't dramatic or obvious at first. But looking back now, I can see it clearly. That choice to honor my soul's nudgings? That was the turning point.

That step out into alignment? It led to the life I have now.

The work that lights me up. The community of students and clients who are doing their own soul work. The teaching that feels like breathing instead of straining. The impact I get to have through helping people understand their own soul agreements and Egbe connections. The financial provision that shows up not through hustle but through alignment. The relationships (friendships, collaborations, connections) that feel like coming home instead of performing.

All of it was waiting on the other side of the truth I'd been afraid to speak.

That's what happens when you honor those quiet (sometimes loud) knowings. When you stop letting fear override your soul agreements. When you trust that Egbe isn't punishing you by closing doors, but redirecting you toward what you actually agreed to.

The doors that closed weren't rejections. They were course corrections. The relationships that fell away weren't failures. They were completions. The life that fell apart wasn't a loss. It was liberation from a path that was never mine to begin with.

And yes, it was hard. Yes, there were moments of doubt and fear and wondering if I'd made a terrible mistake. But even in the hardest moments, there was something underneath the fear—a knowing. A sense that I was finally on the right path, even if that path looked nothing like what I'd been taught to want.

That knowing? That was my Egbe. That was my Enikeji Orun. That was every part of me that remembered what we agreed to before I was born, celebrating the fact that I'd finally stopped running from it.

The life I have now—the work, the purpose, the alignment, the peace that comes from living in integrity with my soul—I couldn't have accessed any of it while I was still lying. While I was still pretending. While I was still choosing comfort over truth.

So when I say your taboos aren't random, when I say they're soul-level information about what your Egbe cannot tolerate in this lifetime, I'm not speaking theoretically.

I'm speaking from the experience of what happens when you honor them. When you trust that your Egbe knows what it's doing. When you choose alignment over ease, truth over comfort, your actual agreements over the life you think you're supposed to want.

The breadcrumbs lead you home. Every single time. You just have to be brave enough to follow them, even when you can't see where they're leading. Even when everyone around you thinks you're making a mistake. Even when it costs you everything you built on the wrong foundation.

Because what's waiting on the other side of that courage? The life you actually came here to live. The work you actually came here to do. The version of yourself that your Egbe has been trying to help you become all along.

That's worth everything it costs. Trust me. I know.

When Egbe Says "It's Time to Go" (Again)

Fast forward a few years. I was working at a university in Florida. On paper, it looked great: stable position, respected institution, steady paycheck, all the things society tells you to aspire to.

But inside, I was dying. Again.

Every day felt harder. The political landscape in Florida was shifting rapidly, especially around education. The dynamics within my department were becoming more stressful. And my spirit was screaming at me, louder and louder: *You have to leave. This is not your path anymore.*

And once again, I didn't listen at first. Because leaving didn't make logical sense. I had bills to pay. I had a reputation to uphold. I had spent years working toward this position. And there were aspects of my job that I absolutely still loved (the students).

So I stayed. And my body started to rebel.

I developed health issues I'd never had before. Digestive problems. Chronic fatigue. Sleep disturbances. At the time, I didn't immediately connect it to the job. But the longer I stayed in that misaligned environment, the worse it got.

Finally, one day, I couldn't do it anymore. My spirit drew a line in the sand and said, *Enough.* I resigned. No backup plan. No financial cushion. Just a deep, bone-level knowing that staying would kill something essential in me.

And you know what happened? Within two to three months of leaving that job, almost all of my health issues cleared up. Not because I started some new diet or wellness routine. But because I stopped forcing my body to hold the weight of a choice my soul had already rejected.

The Body as the Barometer

Your body knows before your mind does.

That's one of the most important lessons I've learned from living in relationship with Egbe. When you're aligned with your agreements, your body feels it. There's ease. Flow. Energy. Things move without excessive force.

When you're out of alignment, your body tells you that too. Through tension. Through illness. Through exhaustion. Through that gnawing feeling in your chest that says, *This isn't right.*

Your Enikeji Orun is trying to communicate with you through your physical form. Your Egbe is orchestrating circumstances to get your attention. Your Ori is signaling that something needs to shift.

The question is: Are you listening?

What Alignment Actually Feels Like

Here's what alignment looked like for me: In 2018, I started doing Akashic Records readings for people. It wasn't a business. It wasn't intentional. It was just one thing leading to the next. Someone would ask for a reading. I'd do it. They'd tell someone else. That person would reach out.

Doors kept unlocking. Opportunities kept appearing. And before I knew it, I looked up in 2019 and realized I had a business: CHI Healing Institute. Not because I planned it. But because I was walking in alignment with what my soul agreed to do.

That's what your Egbe does when you honor your agreements: it clears the path. It orchestrates the synchronicities. It brings the right people at the right time. Not because it's controlling your life, but because it's removing the obstacles that were only there because you were forcing something that wasn't meant for you.

When you're in alignment, one thing naturally leads to the next. Doors open without you having to force them. Things that should be complicated become simple.

And when I finally left my academic position years later, the biggest shift wasn't business opportunities or financial windfalls. It was peace. It was my health returning. It was the ability to breathe without the weight of misalignment crushing my chest.

I left on faith. I left trusting that if I was being called to do this spiritual work on a larger scale, the path would unfold. And it did. Not because the universe rewarded me, but because I was finally walking the path my soul chose before I incarnated.

Helping Others Identify Their Lies

This is why I do the work I do now. Because I know what it's like to live according to programming that isn't yours. I know what it's like to lie to yourself for years because you're afraid of what the truth will cost you.

And I know what freedom feels like on the other side of that honesty.

When I work with clients in the Akashic Records now, one of the first things I look for is: Where are they living according to someone else's truth? Where are they performing instead of being? Where are they honoring societal expectations instead of soul agreements? Where are they carrying ancestral fears that were never theirs to carry? Because until you can identify the lie (the programming, the inherited belief, the false narrative), you can't step into your truth.

And your Egbe? Your Egbe is waiting for you to stop lying to yourself so it can finally work with you instead of constantly trying to redirect you.

The Birth of ASK Programming Work

This is where my work around Ancestral, Societal, and Karmic (ASK) programming was born.

Because what I realized, both through my own experience and through reading thousands of Akashic Records, is that most of us aren't living our soul's truth. We're living someone else's truth that we've mistaken for our own.

Ancestral programming: The beliefs, fears, and traumas passed down through your lineage. The unspoken rules about what's acceptable, what's safe, what's possible.

Societal programming: The cultural narratives about what success looks like, what a good life looks like, what you're supposed to want and be and do.

Karmic programming: The patterns you've carried across lifetimes, the soul contracts you made in other incarnations that are still running in the background.

All of these layers of programming create interference between you and your soul's actual path. They make you think you're choosing when you're actually just reacting. They make you think you're being yourself when you're actually performing a role.

And they keep you stuck in cycles that your soul never agreed to in the first place.

Traditional African divination has always known how to distinguish between soul agreements and inherited patterns. When Ifa reveals that someone's struggles stem from the ancestors or unresolved lineage issues, it's not telling you to change your destiny. It's showing you what's blocking the path to the destiny you already chose.

Here's what divination systems understood long before modern psychology gave us language for it:

- Your Ori chose certain lessons for this lifetime.
- Your ancestors passed down certain patterns: some wisdom, some wounds.
- Society layered on its expectations: what success should look like, who you should be.

These are three different things. And most people are living the last two while thinking they're honoring the first.

The prescribed *ebo* isn't changing your agreements. It's clearing the interference so you can actually walk the path you chose.

Why This Work Matters Beyond You

When you break patterns that have run through your family for generations (addiction, abuse, poverty consciousness, silencing of gifts, fear of visibility) you don't just heal yourself. You heal backward through the lineage, releasing ancestors from patterns they couldn't transform in their lifetimes. And you heal forward, ensuring that children and descendants who come after you won't inherit the same wounds. This is why the work matters beyond your individual life. You're completing work your ancestors started and creating cleaner ground for those who come after you.

Practical Ways to Recognize Your Agreements

So how do you know what your agreements are? How do you figure out what your soul committed to before you took on a body?

Here are some ways I've learned to identify them:

1. Pay attention to what creates friction when you violate it. For me, it was lying to myself about my marriage. I didn't know I had that agreement until I broke it and felt the weight of the dishonesty crushing me. Your agreements often reveal themselves through the consequences of going against them.
2. Notice what feels effortless when you honor it. When I'm doing Akashic Records work, it doesn't feel like work. It feels like breathing. That's because it's aligned with one of my agreements: to help people access their soul-level truth and clear the programming that's blocking them.

3. Look at the patterns that keep showing up. If the same lesson keeps appearing in different forms—relationships, jobs, health issues—that's your Egbe trying to get your attention. The pattern is the agreement asking to be honored.

4. Ask your Egbe directly. Through divination, meditation, journaling, or whatever spiritual practice you use, you can literally ask: What did I agree to? What am I here to do? What values am I meant to embody? And then listen. The answer will come, often in ways you don't expect.

Living the Agreement vs. Knowing the Agreement

Here's the thing: You can know your agreements intellectually and still not live them. That's where most people get stuck.

They do the divination. They read the books. They understand the cosmology. But then they go back to their daily lives and make the same choices they've always made, because living differently feels too hard, too risky, too uncertain.

But your Enikeji Orun doesn't care about your comfort. Your Egbe isn't interested in your excuses. It cares about whether you're honoring what you came here to do.

And when you're not, it will create friction. Not to punish you, but to wake you up.

The Cost and the Reward

Let me be real with you: Living your agreements will cost you something.

It cost me my marriage. It cost me my academic position. It cost me relationships with people who couldn't understand why I was "throwing away" things that looked good on paper.

But what I gained was so much greater.

I gained my soul. I gained the version of myself that my Enikeji Orun had been holding in Orun, waiting for me to remember. I gained the support of my Egbe, which could finally work with me instead of constantly trying to redirect me. I gained the peace that comes from knowing I'm walking the path I chose.

And I gained the ability to help other people do the same.

Closing: The Choice Is Always Yours

Your agreements aren't chains. They're not obligations forced upon you by some external authority. They're choices your soul made because you wanted to grow in these specific ways.

You can honor them, or you can resist them. But either way, they're there. Woven into your Ori. Held by your Enikeji Orun. Witnessed by your Egbe.

And the more you align with them, the more your life opens up.

So start paying attention. To your body. To the patterns. To the synchronicities and the friction. To the quiet voice inside that says, *This way. Not that way.*

That voice? That's your Enikeji Orun, reminding you of what you already know.

That pull? That's your Egbe, calling you home to yourself.

That discomfort when you're lying to yourself? That's your soul speaking truth.

Live your agreements. Not perfectly. Not without stumbling. But honestly. Courageously. Without the lies.

Because that's why you're here.

REFLECTION QUESTIONS

Before you move forward, take time to sit with these questions:

1. Where in your life are you lying to yourself? Where are you performing what you think you should be or do, instead of honoring what your soul actually wants?
2. What societal programming have you absorbed that might not actually be yours? What beliefs about success, relationships, family, or purpose did you inherit rather than choose?
3. When was the last time your body tried to tell you something was wrong? What physical symptoms showed up when you were out of alignment?
4. If you could ask your Enikeji Orun one question right now, what would it be? Write it down. Then sit in stillness and listen for the answer.

CHAPTER 8

UNDERSTANDING YOUR SPIRITUAL RELATIONSHIPS: WHAT THIS CONNECTION ACTUALLY IS

Chapter 7 showed you what alignment looks like when it costs you something. This chapter is about understanding the relationship that sustains you through those costs, and why some friction is actually your soul keeping promises you don't consciously remember making.

Whether you call it Egbe, your soul group, your spiritual family, or the highest version of yourself that exists beyond this incarnation, you have a collective consciousness that holds your pre-birth agreements and actively supports you in living them out.

This principle is universal. Soul groups. Spiritual councils. The communion of saints. Your higher self. The Akashic field. Guardian angels. Ancestors. Each system has its own nuance within the naming and framework, and I'm not suggesting a direct one-to-one translation. But essentially, the names change while the essence remains the same: you're never alone, and consciousness itself is organized to support your evolution.

In this book, I use "Egbe" because that's what this book is about. But everything I'm teaching you in this chapter works whether you ever use that word or not. You don't need initiation into Yoruba tradition to access your soul group. You don't need to adopt a spiritual framework that isn't yours. You need presence, consistency, and honest communication with the consciousness that surrounds you.

In Chapter 5, I gave you practices for recognizing how Egbe is already orchestrating your life. In the Bonus Chapter, I'll give you specific practices for actively building this relationship. But before we get to more practices, I want you to understand what this relationship actually is, what your soul group is doing, and why some of what they do looks like obstacles when it's actually support.

When Soul Agreements Create Earthly Challenges

Let me tell you about a client I'll call Sarafina.

Sarafina was a successful attorney in her late forties who came to me because she couldn't understand why money kept disappearing from her life. Not in small ways. In catastrophic, unexplainable ways.

She'd build substantial wealth, then lose it. Investments that should have been solid would collapse. Business partnerships would dissolve right before the payout. She'd finally get ahead, and then an unexpected lawsuit, a medical emergency, or a failed deal would wipe her out.

This had happened three times over fifteen years. Three times she'd rebuilt from near-zero. Three times she'd gotten close to the financial freedom she craved. Three times something had come along and taken it all.

"I'm not reckless," she told me. "I've analyzed every decision. I've worked with financial advisors, therapists, business coaches. Everyone says I'm doing everything right. So why does this keep happening?"

When I accessed her Akashic Records, the pattern was immediately clear: Sarafina had a soul agreement around wealth and service that she didn't consciously know about.

In a previous lifetime, she'd been wealthy and had used that wealth to cause harm. The specifics aren't important, but what her soul carried forward was a deep, unconscious belief that she couldn't be trusted with abundance. Her Enikeji Orun was running a protective program: *Don't let me accumulate too much. I'll misuse it.*

But here's the complication: In THIS lifetime, Sarafina also had an agreement to heal her relationship with wealth and to use resources for collective good. She chose to build abundance AND steward it responsibly. The two agreements were in tension.

Her Egbe wasn't sabotaging her. Every time she built wealth without conscious awareness of her responsibility to use it for more than personal gain, the money would leave. Her soul wouldn't let her repeat the old pattern.

When I explained this, Sarafina went quiet for a long time.

"So I'm not cursed," she finally said. "I'm being protected from myself."

Yes. And no. She was being held accountable to an agreement she didn't remember making. But the agreement wasn't "never have money." The agreement was "have money AND use it consciously."

The work wasn't about doing a ritual to remove a block. The work was about Sarafina consciously choosing to align her relationship with wealth to her soul's actual agreement. That meant examining her motivations for wanting financial freedom. It meant making commitments about how she'd use resources if they came. It meant healing the past-life wound that made her distrust herself with abundance.

Two years later, Sarafina is more financially stable than she's ever been. Not because the pattern magically disappeared, but because she stopped unconsciously fighting her own agreement. She now runs a foundation alongside her practice. She made conscious commitments about stewardship that her Egbe could witness and trust.

The money stayed because Sarafina finally understood why it kept leaving.

That's what I mean when I say spiritual relationships can feel difficult. Sometimes what looks like an obstacle is actually your Enikeji Orun keeping a promise you don't consciously remember making. Sometimes the friction isn't resistance from your Egbe. It's Egbe's way of showing you there's something deeper you need to address.

The difficulty isn't the problem. The difficulty is the invitation to look deeper.

The Difference Between Transactional and Relational

Before we go further, let me clarify an important distinction.

Transactional spirituality says: I'll give you this offering if you give me that result. I'll light this candle, say this prayer, perform this ritual, and in exchange, you fix my problem.

Relational spirituality says: I'm building connection with you. I'm showing up consistently, listening, honoring your presence in my life, and allowing this relationship to inform how I move through the world.

One treats spiritual forces like cosmic customer service. The other treats them like the soul family they are.

This is the universal principle that Egbe teaches us: consciousness responds to relationship, not manipulation. Whether you're working with

Egbe specifically, your ancestors, your guides, or simply the highest aspect of your own soul, the principle remains the same.

Your soul group isn't here to grant wishes or fix your life while you remain unchanged. They're here to support you in living what you agreed to before birth, but that requires you to show up, pay attention, and do the work of becoming who you came here to be.

If you approach this work with a transactional mindset, you'll be frustrated. If you approach it as relationship building, everything shifts.

What Your Soul Group Is Actually Doing

Your Egbe isn't a cosmic personal assistant waiting to help you manifest your desires, nor is it a panel of judges evaluating your every move.

It is the collective aspect of your own consciousness that exists beyond this single incarnation. It holds the memory of who you are when you forget. It orchestrates circumstances to create opportunities for the growth you agreed to. It creates friction when you drift off-path, not to punish you, but to redirect you.

Think of it this way: before you were born, you made a detailed plan. You knew what you wanted to experience, what you wanted to learn, what gifts you wanted to develop and share, what relationships would catalyze your growth. You made agreements with other souls who would play specific roles in your journey.

Then you drank from the river of forgetfulness and entered a body. The plan didn't disappear. You just stopped consciously remembering it.

Your Egbe remembers.

It's not managing your life from some distant heaven. It IS you, the collective, eternal aspect of you, holding the frequency of your purpose while your human self navigates the density of physical existence.

When doors close repeatedly in a particular direction, that's your Egbe showing you that path isn't aligned with your agreements. When synchronicities lead you somewhere unexpected but exactly right, that's your Egbe orchestrating the set points you agreed to hit. When you feel inexplicably drawn to certain people, places, or work, that's your Egbe activating soul-level recognition.

The relationship isn't about getting Egbe to do things for you. It's about remembering that you are Egbe, expressing in form, and learning to live accordingly.

Why Some Support Looks Like Obstacles

Let me tell you about Marcus.

Marcus was a corporate executive who came to me after his third major career setback in five years. He'd been passed over for promotions he'd earned. He'd had positions eliminated right when he was about to break through. He'd had bosses sabotage his projects for no apparent reason.

"I do everything right," he told me. "I work harder than anyone. I deliver results. And every single time I'm about to reach the next level, something knocks me back down."

When I looked at his Akashic Records, the pattern was clear: Marcus's soul agreement had nothing to do with corporate success. His actual agreement was about teaching, about using his expertise to develop others rather than climbing an organizational ladder for his own advancement.

Every time he got close to "success" as he defined it, his Egbe created friction. Not because it was punishing him, but because the path he was forcing wasn't aligned with his destiny.

"So you're telling me I'm supposed to give up on advancement?" he asked, frustrated.

No. I was telling him to look at what made him feel alive versus what made him feel drained. When he talked about mentoring junior colleagues, his energy shifted completely. When he talked about executive meetings, his body contracted.

His Egbe wasn't blocking his success. It was blocking his detour.

Marcus eventually left corporate life to start a leadership development consultancy. Within a year, he was making more money than he ever had as an executive, and more importantly, he felt aligned. The chronic exhaustion he'd carried for years lifted. The mysterious health issues he'd developed started resolving.

That's what happens when you stop fighting your Egbe and start listening to what it's been showing you all along.

The obstacles weren't obstacles. They were redirections. The friction wasn't punishment. It was precision guidance.

The Foundation Is Presence, Not Performance

I love when people overcomplicate spirituality (insert sarcasm). They think they need special tools, expensive supplies, elaborate altars, perfect timing. And all of that can be beautiful, but it's not required.

Your Egbe doesn't need elaborate ceremony. It needs your presence.

Presence means showing up. Consistently. Authentically. With willingness to listen and follow through on what you hear.

Presence means being honest with yourself about where you're aligned and where you're resisting. It means acknowledging when life is showing you something you don't want to see. It means being willing to make changes that cost you comfort.

What your soul group cares about isn't what you do. It's whether you're willing to be honest about what you already know. Whether you're willing to follow the guidance that's already present in your body, your circumstances, your recurring patterns.

The practices I'll share in the Bonus Chapter aren't magic formulas. They're containers for presence. Ways to focus your attention on the relationship that already exists. Methods for clearing the noise so you can hear what your Egbe has been telling you all along.

How Your Soul Group Communicates

Your soul group is always communicating. The question isn't whether they're speaking. It's whether you're listening.

It speaks in synchronicities, patterns, dreams, body sensations, and what most people dismiss as coincidence. The more you learn its language, the clearer the communication becomes.

Here's what I've learned about how Egbe communicates:

Through repetition. When the same message comes through multiple channels in a short time (someone randomly mentioning exactly what you were thinking about, a book falling off a shelf with exactly the title you needed, a song playing that speaks directly to your situation), that's not coincidence. That's your soul group turning up the volume because you missed the whisper.

Through your body. Your body knows before your mind catches up. That gut feeling, that tension in your shoulders when you're about to agree to something misaligned, that expansion in your chest when you're on the right track: that's your Egbe speaking through your physical form. Your body is part of the communication system.

Through dreams. When your conscious mind is quiet, your soul group can communicate more directly. Not all dreams are messages, but the ones that feel different (more vivid, more urgent, more real than "just a dream") those often carry soul-level information.

Through friction and flow. Where life flows easily, you're likely aligned with your agreements. Where life creates constant friction despite your best efforts, you're likely pushing against your agreements. The friction isn't failure. It's feedback.

Through other people. Sometimes your Egbe will speak through the people around you. The friend who says exactly what you needed to hear. The stranger who gives you a message that changes your direction. The child who asks the question that stops you in your tracks. Your soul group orchestrates these messengers.

Learning to recognize these communications is the foundation of building conscious relationship with your Egbe. In Chapter 5, I gave you practices for noticing the orchestration that's already happening. In the Bonus Chapter, I'll give you practices for actively cultivating the connection and strengthening your ability to receive guidance.

What This Relationship Asks of You

Think about it. You can know your best friend exists. You can have their number saved, know exactly how to reach them. But if you never actually call, if you never check in, if you only reach out when you need something, that's not a relationship. That's an emergency contact.

Your spiritual relationships work the same way. Your Egbe doesn't just want to be acknowledged when you're confused or struggling. It wants to be in relationship with you. Daily. Intimately. As part of the fabric of your life.

Building relationship with your soul group isn't about performing rituals correctly or following formulas precisely. It's about showing up honestly and being willing to change.

What this relationship asks of you:

Honesty. Your Egbe already knows your truth. It witnessed you choose your path before you were born. It knows when you're lying to yourself, when you're settling for less than what you agreed to, when you're hiding behind fear. The relationship deepens when you stop pretending and start being honest about where you are.

Consistency. You don't build relationship through occasional dramatic gestures. You build it through showing up daily. Acknowledging the connection. Paying attention to the guidance. Following through on what you hear. Consistency matters more than intensity.

Willingness to be uncomfortable. Growth happens at the edge of your comfort zone. Your Egbe will guide you toward what you agreed to, and that often means leaving what feels safe. The relationship asks you to trust the discomfort when it's pointing you toward alignment.

Sovereignty, not dependency. Your Egbe supports you. It doesn't make decisions for you. If you're asking it what to have for breakfast, you've gone too far. The relationship is about collaboration, not abdication. You maintain your agency while staying connected to larger guidance.

Action. Your Egbe can orchestrate circumstances, but it can't live your life for you. When you receive guidance, you have to act on it. When you recognize a pattern, you have to be willing to change it. The relationship asks you to move, not just receive.

Moving Into Practice

You now understand what this relationship is: not transactional exchange but ongoing collaboration with the collective aspect of your own consciousness. You understand what your Egbe is doing: holding your agreements, creating circumstances for your growth, redirecting you when you drift off-path. You understand how it communicates: through repetition, your body, dreams, friction and flow, other people.

In the next chapter, we'll explore what it means to live as the intersection between Orun and Aiye, to embody the bridge between spiritual agreements and physical reality.

And in the Bonus Chapter, I'll give you specific daily practices for actively building this relationship: morning alignment, offerings, journaling, dream work, walking meditation, gratitude as recognition, and working with signs. These are the practices that have deepened my own connection with Egbe over the past decade, and they're accessible to anyone regardless of tradition or initiation status.

But remember: practices are containers for presence. The relationship isn't built through doing practices perfectly. It's built through showing up honestly, consistently, and with willingness to change.

Your Egbe is already with you. It's been with you since before you were born. What you're learning isn't how to create the connection. You're learning how to remember it.

You've learned what your Egbe asks of you. You know how it communicates. You understand the difference between transactional and relational spirituality.

But here's what we haven't addressed yet: the assumption underneath all of it.

Throughout this book, I've been using language like "your Egbe" and "connecting with your soul group" as if it's over there and you're over here. As if there's a relationship to build across some kind of distance.

What if that's not quite right?

What if the separation between you and your Egbe isn't a gap to bridge, but an illusion to see through? What if you're not working to align with your Enikeji Orun, but rather, you ARE your Enikeji Orun, experiencing itself in physical form?

That's the recognition that changes everything. And that's where we're going next.

REFLECTION QUESTIONS

Before you move forward, take time to sit with these questions:

1. Where in your life have you experienced what looked like obstacles but might actually have been your Egbe redirecting you away from something misaligned? Looking back, can you see how the "failure" protected you or led you somewhere better?
2. What's your default approach to spirituality: transactional or relational? Do you tend to approach spiritual forces asking for results, or do you approach them as relationships to cultivate regardless of outcome?
3. How does your Egbe typically communicate with you? Through your body? Dreams? Synchronicities? Other people? Which channel do you tend to dismiss or ignore?
4. Where are you currently experiencing friction despite doing "everything right"? What might your Egbe be trying to show you about that situation?
5. Of the five things this relationship asks of you (honesty, consistency, willingness to be uncomfortable, sovereignty, and action), which is your growing edge? Where do you need to develop?

CHAPTER 9

YOU ARE THE BRIDGE: LIVING AS ORUN IN AIYE

There's a moment in every spiritual journey where the seeking stops and the recognizing begins.

You've spent chapters learning the cosmology: Ori choosing destiny, Egbe witnessing your agreements, Enikeji Orun holding the eternal thread. You've seen what embodied alignment looks like when it costs you something. You've been given practices for building conscious relationship with your soul group.

The key here is that you are not separate from any of this.

You are not a human trying to connect with your Egbe in Orun. You are your Enikeji Orun expressing itself in Aiye, carrying Egbe's frequency into form. You are not working to align with your Enikeji Orun. You ARE your Enikeji Orun, experiencing itself in physical form. You are not seeking the Universal Field. You are the Universal Field, localized into this particular body, this particular life, this particular set of agreements.

The bridge between Orun and Aiye that you've been trying to cross? You're standing on it. You've always been standing on it. Because you ARE the bridge.

This chapter is about what shifts when you stop seeking connection and start recognizing what you already are.

The Paradox That Resolves Everything

Let me give you three truths that seem contradictory but are simultaneously and completely accurate:

Truth 1: You are Enikeji Orun: an individuated, eternal soul with your own unique essence, agreements, and evolutionary path. You are distinct. Sovereign. Irreducible to anything else.

Truth 2: You are part of Egbe: a collective soul group that shares resonance, purpose, and pre-birth agreements. You are woven into a web of consciousness that is larger than your individual self.

Truth 3: You are an expression of Universal Consciousness: the infinite field that holds all souls, all possibilities, all dimensions. You are not separate from Source. You ARE Source experiencing itself.

Most spiritual frameworks ask you to choose which of these is true. The individualists say, "You are a unique soul on your own journey." The collectivists say, "You are part of the whole; dissolve your ego." The mystics say, "There is no self; only the One."

Yoruba cosmology, filtered through the lens of universal metaphysics, says: **All three are true. Always. At the same time.** You are singular and plural. Individual and collective. Unique and universal. The paradox isn't a problem to solve. It's the structure of consciousness itself.

Here's the key to holding this paradox: Think fractals.

A fractal is a pattern that repeats at every scale. Zoom in on a fractal, and you see the same structure. Zoom out, and you see it again. The part contains the whole. The whole is expressed through the part. There's no contradiction, just infinite recursion of the same truth at different magnitudes.

That's you.

Your Enikeji Orun is a fractal of your Egbe. Your unique soul essence carries the signature of your soul group. You are individual, yes, but you're individual in a way that perfectly expresses the collective frequency you emerged from. Your Egbe is a fractal of Universal Consciousness. Your soul group carries a specific frequency within the infinite field. Distinct, yes, but never separate from the whole.

And you, in Aiye? You are a fractal of your Enikeji Orun. This human life you're living right now is one expression of your eternal soul self. You are experiencing yourself at a specific density, in a specific time, with specific limitations, but the fullness of who you are has never left Orun.

The Law of Correspondence, "As above, so below," isn't just philosophical poetry. It's fractal geometry. What exists in the infinite field exists in your soul group. What exists in your soul group exists in your eternal self. What exists in your eternal self exists in your human experience.

The pattern repeats. The same truth, at every level. You don't have to choose between individual and collective, personal and universal. You are the place where all of it converges.

And that makes you the bridge.

You Are Not Working With Egbe—You ARE Egbe's Expression

This is the perspective shift that changes everything.

For most of this book, I've used language like "your Egbe" and "connecting with your soul group" because that's where we start, with the sense of relationship between you here and them there. But now I'm going to complicate that.

There is no "you" and "them." There's only consciousness expressing itself in multiple dimensions simultaneously.

When you feel pulled toward creative work that doesn't make logical sense, that's not your Egbe whispering suggestions from Orun. That's Egbe expressing its frequency through you. The impulse IS the message. The desire IS the agreement calling itself into form.

When you experience "random" encounters that shift your entire trajectory (meeting the right person at the right time, stumbling across information exactly when you need it, doors opening that you didn't even know existed) that's not coincidence. That's you, from the Orun aspect of yourself, orchestrating the circumstances that your Aiye self needs to fulfill what you agreed to.

When your body rebels against a relationship that looks perfect on paper, a job that pays well but drains you, a path that everyone says you should take, that's not resistance or self-sabotage. That's Enikeji Orun reminding you who you are. Your body is the messenger. The discomfort is precision guidance.

You aren't receiving signs from somewhere else. You are the sign, manifesting.

Let me get specific, because this can sound abstract. When I knew I needed to leave my marriage in 2016, it wasn't because my Egbe told me to. It was because my Enikeji Orun (the version of me that exists in Orun, the one who chose this life's agreements, the one who knows why I came here) couldn't tolerate the lie anymore. My Aiye self wanted to stay comfortable, avoid judgment, keep the peace. My Enikeji Orun said no. And the friction between those two created so much internal disruption that staying became impossible.

That wasn't guidance from outside. That was me, at the soul level, refusing to abandon the agreements I made.

When you feel the pull toward something that terrifies you (starting the business, writing the book, leaving the career, speaking the truth that will cost you relationships) that's not Egbe pushing you from Orun. That's the fullness of who you are, trying to express itself through the limitations of this human form.

The pull IS the path. The longing IS the agreement. The fear IS the confirmation that you're approaching something your soul chose and your ego wants to avoid.

You aren't trying to align with something external. You're trying to stop resisting what you already are.

When you understand this, the entire spiritual journey shifts.

You stop asking, "What does my Egbe want me to do?" and start asking, "What am I refusing to acknowledge that I already know?"

You stop waiting for signs to make things obvious and start trusting the quiet knowing that's been there all along.

You stop treating your desires like distractions from your spiritual path and start recognizing them as the path itself, calling you home.

Because you aren't separate from your soul group. You are your soul group's presence in physical form. Every impulse, every longing, every inexplicable pull: that's it. That's you. Same thing.

The work isn't to connect with Egbe. The work is to stop pretending you're not already Egbe, walking around in a body, trying to remember why you came here.

Living as the Intersection

If you are the bridge between Orun and Aiye, then you exist in both realms simultaneously.

Not metaphorically. Not "part of you here, part of you there." You, all of you, exist in multiple dimensions at once. Right now. Always.

In Yoruba cosmology, we say everyone has their Enikeji Orun, their spiritual double in heaven. But the language of "double" can be misleading because it implies separation. Like you're down here and your twin is up there, and you're trying to communicate across distance.

That's not what's happening.

You are not split. You are simultaneous. The you that exists in Orun and the you that exists in Aiye are the same consciousness, experiencing itself at different densities. Think of it like water and ice—same substance, different states. You didn't leave part of yourself in Orun when you incarnated. You condensed into form while remaining fully present in formlessness.

This is what it means to be the bridge. You are the living intersection where the unseen becomes seen, where agreements held in the spiritual realm seek expression through physical choices, where the infinite funnels itself into the finite without ever becoming less than infinite.

What does this mean practically?

It means every choice you make in Aiye ripples into Orun. Every agreement held in Orun seeks expression through your Aiye choices. There is no separation between your spiritual life and your human life. There is only one life, experienced across dimensions.

When you honor your body's knowing, you're honoring Enikeji Orun speaking through density.

When you follow the pull toward work that lights you up, you're allowing Egbe to express its frequency in form.

When you release relationships that drain you, you're clearing space for the connections that actually align with your soul group's resonance.

When you speak truth that costs you comfort, you're living the agreement that your Ori chose before you were born.

This is what "As above, so below" means at its deepest level.

It's not that Orun influences Aiye like some distant force pulling strings. It's that Orun and Aiye are the same consciousness in different states, and you are the place where those states meet. The boundary between them isn't a wall—it's you. The bridge isn't something you walk across. It's what you are.

Let me give you an example.

When I went to Osogbo, I thought I was going to Nigeria to receive something—knowledge, power, confirmation, connection with my spiritual family. And I did receive all of that. But what I didn't understand then, and what I understand now, is that I wasn't going to Orun to meet my Egbe. I was going to Aiye to remember that I never left them.

The ritual didn't create the connection. It revealed what was already true. My Egbe has been with me since before I was born. It witnessed my agreements. It's been orchestrating my path, clearing obstacles, creating friction when I drift off-course. Not because it's a separate entity managing my life from heaven, but because I am Egbe, experiencing this particular incarnation, and the fullness of who I am keeps the human part of me connected.

The initiation ceremony made that visible. The priest called it forward, named my class of Egbe, identified the taboos, consecrated the shrine. But all of that was recognition, not creation. I was always Egbe. I just needed the ritual to make it conscious.

That's what living as the intersection looks like. You don't become the bridge. You recognize you've always been the bridge. And then you start living accordingly.

Your relationships mirror your soul agreements because the people you're drawn to are expressions of the frequency you carry. You didn't accidentally meet them. Your Orun self and their Orun self recognized the resonance, and circumstances aligned to bring your Aiye selves together. That's Egbe at work. That's orchestration.

Your creative work manifests Orun frequency because what you create in Aiye is an echo of what exists in the spiritual realm. The song you can't stop hearing, the book you need to write, the business idea that won't leave you alone—those aren't random impulses. It's Egbe pressing through, trying to bring into form what was agreed upon before form.

Your struggles are Egbe creating friction to wake you up because when you're living out of alignment (performing someone else's path, hiding your gifts, shrinking to fit spaces too small for your soul) the discomfort you feel isn't punishment. It's precision guidance. Your Enikeji Orun is using pain as a homing signal, pointing you back toward truth.

Your joy is confirmation you're living what you chose because alignment feels like homecoming. Not ease—living your agreements often costs you comfort, relationships, security. But even in the difficulty, there's a rightness. A resonance. A sense of "Yes, this. Exactly this. This is why I came."

That feeling? That's you in Aiye recognizing you in Orun. The bridge experiencing itself from both sides.

The Responsibility of Being the Bridge

With this recognition comes responsibility.

If you are Egbe expressing in form, if you are Enikeji Orun experiencing itself in density, if you are Universal Consciousness localized into this particular body and life, then you cannot outsource your evolution to spiritual forces.

Because you ARE the spiritual force.

It doesn't rescue you. It IS you, calling yourself home.

Let me be clear: This doesn't mean you're alone. You are held by consciousness at every level. Your Egbe supports you because you're part of it. Your ancestors guide you because your success is their success. The Orisa align you because you carry their principles within you. Source holds you because you ARE Source experiencing itself through this particular configuration of form.

But none of them will live your life for you. That's your job. The only job, actually.

You cannot wait for Egbe to make your path obvious while you stay in situations that are killing your spirit.

You cannot ask Enikeji Orun for signs while ignoring the ones your body has been giving you for years.

You cannot pray to Source for clarity while refusing to face the truth you already know.

The spiritual work isn't to figure out your agreements. The spiritual work is to live them even when it's terrifying, costly, and inconvenient.

When you understand that you are the bridge, certain questions stop making sense:

"What does my Egbe want me to do?" becomes "What am I refusing to acknowledge that I already know?"

"How do I connect with my higher self?" becomes "What am I doing that's disconnecting me from my own truth?"

"Why isn't Source answering my prayers?" becomes "What am I asking Source to do that I'm supposed to do myself?"

This is spiritual sovereignty. Not the kind that says "I don't need anyone." The kind that says "I am not separate from the consciousness that guides me, so I can trust my own knowing."

You aren't waiting for permission from Orun to live what you chose in Orun. You're just waiting for your Aiye self to stop resisting what your Enikeji Orun already knows.

What does this look like in practice?

It looks like making the phone call you've been avoiding for months because your body tenses every time you think about it. That tension is Enikeji Orun saying, "This relationship is done. Honor it."

It looks like quitting the job that pays your bills but drains your soul, even when you don't have the next thing lined up. Because the pull toward something else is so strong that staying feels like dying slowly. That pull is Egbe orchestrating your path. Trust it.

It looks like starting the creative project that terrifies you because you know it will expose you, make you vulnerable, invite judgment. But the need to create it is louder than the fear. That need is your agreement manifesting. Let it.

It looks like telling the truth that will cost you relationships, comfort, security, because continuing to lie costs you yourself. And you are Egbe. You cannot abandon you.

This is what it means to live as the bridge. Every choice either honors the consciousness you are or denies it. There's no neutral. Every moment is alignment or resistance.

And here's the thing: your Egbe is patient, but not passive. If you ignore the gentle nudges long enough, the nudges become shoves. The whispers become shouts. The discomfort becomes crisis.

Not because your soul group is punishing you. Because it loves you too much to watch you waste this incarnation living someone else's agreements.

When crisis arrives, when foundations crack without warning, pause before panic. Ask: "What have I been refusing to see? What truth have I been avoiding? What agreement have I been denying?"

The destruction might be Enikeji Orun refusing to let you build on a foundation that was never yours. Sometimes the ground must be cleared before the right structure can emerge.

And when you finally stop resisting, when you make the change, speak the truth, honor the knowing, live the agreement, the chaos settles. Not immediately. Realignment takes time. But the frantic energy shifts. Peace becomes possible again. Doors start opening.

That's how you know you're living as the bridge instead of resisting it.

The external circumstances might still be hard (living your agreements often is) but internally, something settles. You stop feeling split. You stop performing. You stop pretending. You just live.

And that's when Egbe can actually work through you, instead of having to work around your resistance to yourself.

Integration Through Choice

Let's bring this down to the ground. Because recognition is beautiful, but recognition without application is just philosophy.

You are the bridge between Orun and Aiye. You are Egbe expressing in form. You are Enikeji Orun experiencing density. You are consciousness meeting itself.

What does that mean when you wake up tomorrow morning?

It means every choice you make is either honoring the bridge or denying it. Living what you agreed to or performing what others expect. Expressing your truth or hiding it to keep the peace.

There is no neutral. Every moment is alignment or resistance.

This isn't about perfection. You're going to resist. You're going to choose comfort over truth, security over soul, approval over authenticity. You're human. That's allowed.

But you need to know that's what you're doing. Own the resistance when it happens. Don't spiritualize it, don't make excuses for it, don't pretend you didn't have a choice. You always have a choice. And sometimes the honest choice is: "I know this isn't aligned, but I'm choosing it anyway because I'm not ready."

That's fine. Just don't lie to yourself about it. Because lying to yourself is the one thing Egbe cannot tolerate. Remember Chapter 7? That was my taboo. I can compromise. I can delay. I can choose the comfortable path over the aligned one, as long as I'm honest that that's what I'm doing. But the moment I lie to myself about it, my life falls apart.

Your taboo might be different. But the principle is the same. Self-honesty is the foundation of living as the bridge. Because you cannot honor agreements you refuse to acknowledge.

So the practice is simple: Pay attention to the choice in front of you, and ask yourself which direction it's pointing.

Is this choice moving me toward truth or away from it? Toward my gifts or away from them? Toward my knowing or away from it?

That's it. That's the whole compass.

You already know the answer. Your body knows. Your energy knows. The tightness in your chest when you think about staying in that relationship—that's knowing. The way time disappears when you're doing that creative work—that's knowing. The inexplicable pull toward that city, that person, that path—that's knowing.

You don't need more information. You need to trust what you already have.

The questions from Chapter 8 become your daily practice now:

"Am I aligned right now?"

"Is this choice honoring my agreements?"

"What am I resisting that I need to see?"

Ask them throughout the day. Not as spiritual performance, but as genuine check-in. And then listen. Your Enikeji Orun will answer. Every time.

Sometimes the answer is, "Yes, stay. This is hard, but it's yours." Sometimes the answer is, "No. Leave. This was never meant for you." Sometimes the answer is, "Not yet. You're building something. Trust the process."

The answer will come through your body, your energy, your resonance. Learn to distinguish between fear (which is old programming, trauma responses, ego protection trying to keep you small and safe) and soul-level knowing (which is Enikeji Orun speaking, even when it's uncomfortable).

Fear feels constricting. Tight. Based in "what if." It closes you down, makes you smaller, keeps you stuck.

Soul-level knowing feels clarifying. Even when it's grief, or loss, or hard truth, it opens something. It expands your capacity. It moves you toward more of yourself, not less.

When you feel resistance in your body, pause. Hand on your chest or your head. Breathe. Ask: "Is this fear speaking, or is this my soul showing me I'm off-path?"

Then trust what comes. The first hit is usually right. It's the second-guessing, the rationalizing, the "but what will people think"—that's when you start lying to yourself.

The bridge doesn't require elaborate ritual. It doesn't need perfect conditions. It doesn't wait for you to have it all figured out.

The bridge just asks you to be honest about what you know, honor what you feel, and make choices that align with the agreements you made before you forgot you made them.

That's the practice. Every day. Every choice. Every moment.

Am I living as the bridge, or am I pretending I'm separate from the consciousness that guides me?

Am I expressing Egbe in form, or am I performing someone else's idea of who I should be?

Am I honoring Enikeji Orun, or am I overriding my knowing to stay comfortable?

The answer determines everything.

What Comes Next

You aren't seeking the bridge. You ARE the bridge. You are Egbe expressing in form, Enikeji Orun experiencing density, consciousness meeting itself in the particularity of your life.

This recognition changes how you approach everything that comes next. But it also raises new questions.

If you are your Enikeji Orun expressing in this body, what has your eternal soul self been carrying across lifetimes? What patterns, wounds, and gifts did you bring into this incarnation from before? And how do those multi-lifetime agreements interact with what your Ori chose specifically for this life?

The bridge doesn't just connect Orun and Aiye in this moment. It connects this lifetime to all the others your soul has lived. Understanding that continuity is essential to understanding who you really are and what you came here to complete.

In Part IV, we expand the lens. The next chapter explores what your Enikeji Orun carries across incarnations and how to recognize the agreements that are older than this body. Then we move into practical territory: specific methods for discovering YOUR agreements, not just understanding the system but knowing your particular place within it.

The bridge has been recognized. Now it's time to see how far it extends.

REFLECTION QUESTIONS

Before you move forward, take time to sit with these questions:

1. Where in your life have you been treating yourself as separate from your soul group, waiting for guidance from "them" instead of recognizing your deepest impulses as Egbe expressing through you?
2. What truth have you been avoiding because you are waiting for external confirmation, even though your body has been giving you the answer for months or years?
3. If you fully accepted that you are the bridge between Orun and Aiye, that your choices here ripple into the spiritual realm and your agreements there seek expression through your life now, what would you do differently tomorrow?
4. What one choice are you facing right now where you already know the aligned answer, but you are resisting it? What would it cost you to honor that knowing? What would it cost you to continue denying it?

PART IV

EXPANSION

You've learned the cosmology. You've seen the correspondence between spiritual agreements and physical life. You've practiced embodiment and built conscious relationship with your soul group. You know what it means to live as the bridge.

Now we expand the lens.

Part IV stretches everything you've learned across time, across lifetimes, and into the practical specifics of YOUR unique soul path. This is where we address the questions you've been building toward since Chapter 1: What are MY specific agreements? How do I discover what I actually came here to do? And how do I sustain this work for the long term?

In the chapters ahead, you'll explore the eternal thread: how your Enikeji Orun carries patterns, wisdom, and agreements across multiple incarnations. You will learn practical methods for discovering your specific soul agreements through pattern recognition, divination, body wisdom, and what your life is already showing you. And you'll get clear guidance on walking this path forward, living soul-aligned in a world that was not built for it.

This is the practical payoff. This is where everything comes together. You are ready.

CHAPTER 10

THE ETERNAL THREAD: ENIKEJI ORUN ACROSS LIFETIMES

Now that you recognize you ARE the bridge, let us expand the lens to see what you've been bridging across. Not just this lifetime, but all of them.

Chapter 9 ended with a recognition: you are Egbe expressing in form, Enikeji Orun experiencing density, consciousness meeting itself. That recognition changes everything about how you relate to your spiritual work in the present.

But there's more to understand. Because if you are the bridge between Orun and Aiye, if you are consciousness localized into this particular body, then death isn't an ending. It is a transition. A shift in state. Water becoming vapor.

We Need to Talk About What Happens After You Die

Or more accurately: what happens before you were born, what is happening while you are living, and what continues after this body stops working.

This chapter is where I complicate everything you've learned so far. Not to confuse you, but to expand the frame. Because Egbe and Enikeji Orun don't just operate within this one lifetime. They operate across all of them.

Traditional Yoruba cosmology focuses on this incarnation. When your Ori chose destiny at Àjàlá's house, when your Egbe witnessed your agreements, when you descended into Aiye, that is the story. The emphasis is on living this life well, honoring your Ori's choice, fulfilling what you came here to do, and eventually returning to Orun.

But through my work in the Akashic Records, through years of spiritual practice across multiple traditions, through paying attention to patterns that repeat across generations and relationships and circumstances, I've come to understand something more. Your Enikeji Orun, your eternal soul self, doesn't start when you are born and end when you die. It is the thread that runs through multiple incarnations, carrying forward what has not been resolved, what has not been learned, what has not been expressed.

This isn't a contradiction of Yoruba cosmology. It's an expansion of it through the lens of universal metaphysics. And it changes everything about how you understand your agreements, your relationships, your struggles, and your purpose.

I want to be clear: this is my interpretation and synthesis, informed by my work in the Akashic Records and across multiple traditions. I'm not claiming traditional authority. I am sharing what spirit has revealed to me through years of practice.

What Traditional Yoruba Cosmology Teaches

Let me start by honoring what the tradition says, because I'm not here to override Yoruba cosmology with Western metaphysical concepts. I'm here to show you how they are describing the same truth from different angles.

Traditional Yoruba practice doesn't spend much time on questions about what happens across multiple lifetimes because the emphasis is practical: Live this life well. Honor your destiny. Appease your Egbe. Support your lineage. What happens across multiple lifetimes matters less than what you're doing right now.

And that's beautiful. That is grounding. That keeps spiritual practice focused on embodied action rather than abstract philosophy.

But when I started working in the Akashic Records, when I began accessing information about patterns that clearly predated this lifetime, agreements that felt older than this incarnation, soul connections that transcended this body, I could not ignore what I was seeing. Your Enikeji Orun, your eternal soul self, carries more than this life. It carries the accumulated wisdom, wounds, gifts, and unfinished work of multiple incarnations.

And your Egbe? It has been with you through all of them.

How the Akashic Records Showed Me the Long View

The Akashic Records do not operate within the framework of a single lifetime. When you access someone's Records, you're not just seeing this incarnation. You are seeing the eternal thread, the soul's journey across time, space, and form.

That is how I started to understand that Enikeji Orun does not begin and end with this body. It is the continuity. The self that was before you were born, that exists while you are here, and that continues after you die.

In the Records, I have seen patterns that make no sense in the context of this lifetime alone:

A client with an inexplicable fear of abandonment, despite having loving, present parents. The Records showed a past-life pattern of being left behind repeatedly, creating a soul-level wound her Enikeji Orun carried into this life.

A client who effortlessly excelled at teaching complex spiritual concepts, despite minimal formal training. The Records revealed multiple past incarnations as a priest, mystic, and spiritual teacher. Her Enikeji Orun brought mastery forward.

A client struggling with the same toxic relationship dynamic across multiple partners. The Records showed an unresolved agreement from a past life to learn boundaries and self-worth: work her Enikeji Orun was still completing.

These are not isolated cases. This is how the soul works. Your Enikeji Orun does not forget. It carries forward what needs healing, what needs expressing, what needs completing. And your Egbe, your soul group, witnesses all of it, supporting you across lifetimes as you evolve.

This expanded my understanding of Yoruba cosmology. Ori chooses destiny for this lifetime. Enikeji Orun carries the eternal thread across lifetimes. Egbe witnesses both.

It is not contradiction. It is layers of truth.

How to Recognize What Your Enikeji Orun Is Carrying

If your Enikeji Orun carries agreements and patterns across lifetimes, how do you know what is from before? How do you distinguish between what you are healing from this life and what you are carrying from previous ones?

Here are the markers I have learned to recognize:

Inexplicable Mastery. If you are unnaturally good at something despite minimal training or experience, that is likely your Enikeji Orun bringing forward mastery from a past life. You pick up an instrument and within weeks you're playing at an intermediate level. You start teaching and people immediately respond to your guidance, even though you're new to it. You write, paint, heal, lead, create, and it flows effortlessly, like you're remembering rather than learning. That is not talent. That is mastery your soul developed before. Your Enikeji Orun is expressing what it already knows.

Irrational Fears. If you have a fear that makes no sense given your life experience, that is likely your Enikeji Orun carrying forward a wound from before. You're terrified of water despite never having a traumatic water experience. You panic in enclosed spaces despite never being trapped. You have nightmares about abandonment despite having secure relationships. These aren't random. They're your soul remembering what happened before and trying to protect you from re-experiencing it. The work isn't to dismiss these fears as irrational. The work is to acknowledge them, heal them, and release your Enikeji Orun from carrying them forward.

Instant Recognition. When you meet someone and feel like you've known them forever, that is your Enikeji Orun recognizing a soul you've incarnated with before. This happens with romantic partners, with close friends, sometimes even with people you meet briefly who leave an outsized impact on your life. The familiarity isn't imagination. It's your soul recognizing another soul it has traveled with across lifetimes. Your Egbe often orchestrates these meetings because it knows certain souls need to reconnect to complete unfinished work, heal old wounds, or support each other's evolution. Pay attention to who feels familiar. They're probably part of your soul's larger story.

Repeating Patterns. If the same dynamic keeps showing up across different people, different contexts, different phases of your life, that pattern is probably older than this incarnation. You keep attracting emotionally unavailable partners, despite working on yourself, despite choosing different types. You keep experiencing betrayal in friendships, despite being loyal and trustworthy yourself. You keep sabotaging success right before breakthrough, despite wanting to succeed. These aren't character flaws. They are agreements your Enikeji Orun is working on across lifetimes. The pattern repeats because the work isn't done yet. Your job is not to beat yourself up for not "fixing" it. Your job is to engage with the healing work consciously, knowing this might be a multi-lifetime agreement.

Body Knowing. Your body carries soul memory. Sometimes the most direct way to access what your Enikeji Orun is holding is through somatic awareness. Pay attention to what your body tells you. If you feel instant calm in a place you've never been, that might be your soul recognizing a location from another incarnation. If certain music moves you to tears for reasons you cannot explain, that might be your Enikeji Orun remembering. The body does not lie. It remembers what the conscious mind has forgotten.

The Danger of Past-Life Obsession

Before we go further, I need to give you a warning: don't get so obsessed with past lifetimes that you forget to live this one.

I've seen too many people use past-life exploration as spiritual bypassing, avoiding the work they need to do now by blaming everything on what happened before. "I can't trust people because I was betrayed in a past life." "I'm broke because I took a vow of poverty as a monk." "My relationship is struggling because we were enemies in another incarnation."

Maybe. Or maybe you're just not doing the healing work required in this lifetime.

Past-life information is useful when it helps you understand patterns so you can address them. It's harmful when it becomes an excuse to avoid responsibility for your current choices.

Your Enikeji Orun carries forward unresolved wounds, yes. But you have agency in this lifetime. You can choose to heal what was broken. You can choose to release what's no longer serving you. You can choose to complete what was left undone.

That's why you incarnated. Not to passively carry forward the past, but to actively transform it.

So if you're going to explore past incarnations (through the Akashic Records, through meditation, through any method), do it with the intention of resolution, not fascination. Ask: "What is my Enikeji Orun carrying that needs healing in this lifetime?" Then do the work to heal it.

Don't just collect past-life stories like spiritual credentials. Use the information to become more whole in this life.

Why We Forget What We Chose

The river of forgetfulness, omi igbagbe in Yoruba, that souls cross before birth is not punishment. It's protection. It preserves the operational reality of free will.

If you consciously remembered all your past lives, your soul's entire history of agreements and patterns, this life would become performance of a known script rather than authentic choice-making. You would be acting out what you already know instead of genuinely choosing in each moment.

The forgetting creates the possibility for real evolution. You have to find your way home without a map, which is precisely what makes the journey meaningful and the growth authentic.

But the forgetting isn't total.

Your Enikeji Orun retains the wisdom even when your conscious mind doesn't. Your body carries soul memory. Your inexplicable talents, irrational fears, instant recognitions: these are your eternal soul self breaking through the veil, reminding you of what you've been before and what you're working on across lifetimes.

This is why divination exists. Ifa pierces the veil, accessing Orunmila's witness to show you what you don't consciously remember but your Enikeji Orun has never forgotten.

Your Egbe Across Lifetimes

This is where everything we've been building comes together:

Your Egbe isn't just your soul group in this lifetime. It is your soul group across all lifetimes.

The consciousness you share frequency with, the agreements you made before incarnation, the collective that witnesses your evolution: it's continuous. When you die and return to Orun, you return to it. When you incarnate again, it witnesses your new Ori's choice and supports you through another expression.

It doesn't change. The form changes, the specific agreements change, the context changes, but the soul group remains.

This is why Egbe work is so powerful. You're not just building relationship with spiritual forces for this one lifetime. You're strengthening a connection that transcends incarnation. The relationship you cultivate with your Egbe now will still be there when you transition. And it was there before you were born.

It has been with you through every incarnation. It has witnessed every version of you: the king and the pauper, the healer and the wounded, the oppressor and the oppressed, the creator and the destroyer. It has seen you at your highest expression and your lowest moment. It has celebrated your breakthroughs and mourned your failures.

And it's still here. Still supporting you. Still orchestrating circumstances to help you complete what you came to do.

Because that is what soul groups do. They don't abandon you when you make mistakes. They don't withdraw when you fail. They don't judge you when you forget. They just keep showing up, lifetime after lifetime, creating the conditions for your evolution.

That's unconditional support. Not in the "I'll rescue you from consequences" sense, but in the "I'll never stop believing you can complete what you agreed to" sense.

The Agreements That Span Lifetimes

Some agreements you make with your Egbe are specific to one incarnation. "In this life, I am going to be a teacher." "In this life, I'm going to heal the mother wound in my lineage." "In this life, I'm going to create art that shifts consciousness."

Those are Ori-level agreements, specific to the destiny you chose for this particular incarnation.

But some agreements are Enikeji Orun-level. They span multiple lifetimes because the work is too vast to complete in one.

"I'm going to master the balance between power and compassion." That might take five incarnations. "I'm going to heal the ancestral pattern of addiction in my lineage." That might take seven lifetimes, playing different roles, approaching it from different angles. "I'm going to contribute to the evolution of collective consciousness." That might take dozens of incarnations, each one adding a thread to the larger tapestry.

Your Egbe witnesses all of it: the single-lifetime agreements and the multi-lifetime ones. It supports both. And it knows which is which, even when you don't.

This is why some work feels urgent and other work feels eternal. The urgent work is what you came to do in this specific incarnation. The eternal work is what your Enikeji Orun is carrying across multiple lives.

Both matter. But you navigate them differently.

The urgent work requires focused action in this lifetime. Do it now. Do not wait. This is your Ori's path. Live it.

The eternal work requires patience, trust, and the willingness to contribute your piece without needing to see the whole picture. You might not complete it in this lifetime. That's okay. Your Enikeji Orun will carry it forward. Your Egbe will support the next iteration.

The key is knowing which you're working on. And trusting that both are held.

Living With the Long View

When you understand that your Enikeji Orun carries agreements across lifetimes, it changes how you relate to time, struggle, and success.

You stop treating this lifetime like it is the only chance you have to get everything right. It's not. It's one expression of your eternal soul's evolution. Do your best. Live your agreements. Use your gifts. Heal what you can. But don't destroy yourself trying to achieve perfection in one incarnation.

You stop judging yourself so harshly when patterns repeat. Of course they repeat. You are working on agreements that are older than this lifetime. The fact that you are still struggling doesn't mean you're failing. It means you're engaged with deep work that requires multiple attempts.

You stop resenting the people who trigger your wounds. They're probably soul family, showing up to help you heal what your Enikeji Orun is carrying. The friction isn't random. It's orchestrated. By them, by you, by the agreements you both made before incarnation.

You start seeing your life as one chapter in a much larger story. What you are building here: the healing, the growth, the mastery, the love. It doesn't end when this body dies. Your Enikeji Orun carries it forward. Your Egbe continues supporting it. The work continues.

That's both humbling and liberating.

Humbling because you realize you're not going to "finish" everything in this lifetime. The work is bigger than one incarnation.

Liberating because you can stop trying to force completion and start trusting the process. Do what you can in this life. Your Enikeji Orun will carry the rest. Your Egbe will support the continuation.

You are held across time. You always have been. You always will be.

From Understanding to Discovery

You now understand the long view. You know that your Enikeji Orun carries patterns, wounds, gifts, and agreements across lifetimes. You know that your Egbe has been with you through all of them. You know the difference between urgent, this-lifetime work and eternal, multi-incarnation work.

But understanding the system is one thing. Knowing your specific place within it is another.

You've been asking the question since Chapter 1: "What are MY specific agreements?" Let me show you how to find them.

REFLECTION QUESTIONS

Before you move forward, take time to sit with these questions:

1. What patterns, fears, or inexplicable abilities in your life might be carried forward from previous incarnations? What does your Enikeji Orun seem to be working on across lifetimes?
2. How does understanding multi-lifetime agreements change how you relate to your current struggles? What feels more patient, more compassionate, more spacious?
3. Which of your current life challenges feel like urgent, this-lifetime work? Which feel like the eternal work your soul is carrying across incarnations?
4. What ancestral patterns do you see returning through your family? What role might you be playing in healing, completing, or continuing that work?
5. If you knew you were working on agreements that span multiple lifetimes, how would that change your relationship with "success" and "failure" in this incarnation?

CHAPTER 11

DISCOVERING YOUR AGREEMENTS: HOW TO KNOW WHAT YOU CAME HERE TO DO

I know what you're thinking right now.

You've spent ten chapters learning about Ori choosing destiny, Egbe witnessing your agreements, Enikeji Orun carrying patterns across lifetimes, and the Universal Field holding all of it. You understand the cosmology. You've seen what embodied alignment looked like for me. You have practices for building relationship with your soul group.

But you're sitting there asking: "Okay, but what are MY specific agreements? What did I actually come here to do?"

That's the question this chapter answers.

Because understanding the system is one thing. Knowing your specific place within it is another. And you can't fully live your agreements until you know what they are.

The good news? You don't have to guess. Your agreements aren't hidden in some inaccessible spiritual vault. They're woven through your entire life: in the patterns that repeat, in the gifts that come naturally, in the wounds that will not heal, in the longings that won't quiet, in the people who keep showing up.

Your life IS the revelation. You just need to learn how to read it.

Your Life Is Already Showing You Your Agreements

Before we get to formal methods like the Akashic Records or Ifa divination, I want you to understand something essential: you don't need external confirmation to know what you came here to do. Your life has been showing you all along.

The patterns that repeat across your relationships, your jobs, your challenges, your breakthroughs: those aren't random. They're curriculum. Your Egbe has been orchestrating circumstances to show you, repeatedly, what you're working on.

So before you seek answers from anywhere else, look at what your life is already telling you.

What Themes Keep Repeating? Look back at your entire life. What shows up again and again, regardless of the specific context? Maybe every job you have had, no matter how different they seem, has required you to bring order to chaos. Maybe every relationship has taught you something about boundaries or trust or vulnerability. Maybe you keep being put in positions where you have to speak difficult truths. The repeating theme is the curriculum. It's what your soul keeps returning to because that's what you came to learn or demonstrate.

What Comes Naturally? Your gifts are not accidents. The things that come effortlessly to you, that feel like breathing instead of straining, those are agreements. You agreed to bring those capacities into this lifetime and use them. If you can hold space for people's pain without being destroyed by it, that's a gift. If you can see patterns and systems that others miss, that's a gift. If you can translate complex ideas into accessible language, that's a gift. What do you do that feels like breathing? That's probably part of why you're here.

What Breaks You Open? This one is harder to accept, but it's true: your deepest wounds are often directly connected to your deepest agreements. Not because your soul wants you to suffer. But because the wounds you carry, whether from this lifetime or carried forward by your Enikeji Orun, point to what you came to transform, both for yourself and for the collective. If you experienced abandonment and spent your life learning how to belong to yourself first, your agreement might be healing the abandonment wound in your lineage or teaching others how to find home within themselves. The wound becomes the medicine when you transform it instead of just surviving it. Look at your life's deepest pain points. Not to wallow in them, but to ask: What did this force me to develop? What capacity did I build because of this struggle? And who might need what I learned?

Who Keeps Appearing? Pay attention to who shows up in your life repeatedly. Not just the people who stay, but the TYPES of people who appear. Do you consistently attract people who need healing? That might signal an agreement to be a healer, a space-holder, a teacher. Do you consistently attract people who challenge your boundaries? That might signal an agreement to master self-protection, to learn when to say no. The people aren't random. Your Egbe orchestrates these encounters because they're part of your curriculum. Even the difficult relationships, especially the difficult relationships, are often soul family showing up to help you learn what you came to master.

What Won't Leave You Alone? And then there's the thing you cannot stop thinking about. The creative project that's been haunting you for years. The career shift you keep dismissing as impractical. The book you're supposed to write. The business you're supposed to start. The pull that persists despite obstacles, despite logic, despite everyone telling you it's not realistic: that's an agreement, screaming. Your Egbe doesn't whisper once and then give up. It orchestrates repetition. If something keeps calling you, across years, through different circumstances, even when you try to ignore it: that's not random obsession. That is your soul, trying to get your attention.

Methods for Accessing Your Agreements Directly

Your life shows you your agreements through pattern. But if you want more specific information (confirmation, clarity, details about how to move forward) there are multiple pathways for accessing that knowledge directly.

Not everyone has the same access points. Some people can afford divination. Some can't. Some people are initiated into tradition. Some aren't. Some people have strong intuitive channels. Some are still developing them.

So I'm going to give you multiple methods. Use what's accessible to you. Trust what resonates. And remember: you don't need ALL of these. You just need ONE that works.

Through the Akashic Records. The Akashic Records are the energetic archive of every soul's journey: every agreement made, every lifetime lived, every choice taken, every possibility held. When you access your Records, you can ask directly about what you came to do in this incarnation.

I've written extensively about how to access the Akashic Records in my previous book, *Accessing the Akashic Records: A Practical Guide to Healing, Clarity, and Empowerment* (2024). If this methodology calls to you, that book will give you the full protocol. When you open your Records, you can ask specific questions: "What are my primary soul agreements in this lifetime?" "What gifts did I agree to express?" "What am I here to heal?" "What relationships are part of my soul agreements?" The information comes in different forms depending on how you receive: images, words, emotions, body sensations, or direct knowing. However it comes for you is correct. Trust it.

Through Ifa Divination. If you're working within Yoruba tradition or feel called to it, Ifa divination is another system for understanding your Ori's path and your soul agreements. Ifa doesn't use the language of "past lives" or "multi-lifetime soul evolution" the way Western metaphysics does, but it does reveal: what destiny your Ori chose, what Orisa walk with you, what your life's purpose is, what obstacles you'll face and how to navigate them, what taboos you need to honor. A skilled Babalawo (Ifa priest) or Iyanifa (Ifa priestess) can cast the *opele* (divination chain) or *ikin* (sacred palm nuts) and read the *Odu*, the sacred verses that speak directly to your situation. If you go this route, find a legitimate priest rooted in tradition, not someone who learned Ifa from a weekend workshop or a book. Be prepared to make the *ebos* (offerings/sacrifices) prescribed. Understand that Ifa divination is relational, not transactional.

Through Body Wisdom and Resonance. This method is accessible to everyone. Your body already knows your agreements. It responds to alignment with ease, flow, energy. It responds to misalignment with tension, depletion, illness. You don't need external divination to access this information. You just need to pay attention to what your body tells you. The Resonance Test: Think about different possibilities for your life. As you think about each one, notice what happens in your body. Does your chest open or close? Does your breathing deepen or shallow? Does energy rise or drop? Your body's response tells you what's aligned. Learn to distinguish between the tightness of fear (which is ego protection) and the tightness of misalignment (which is your soul saying no). Fear feels like: "This is scary but I want to do it anyway. I'm terrified but also alive." Misalignment feels like: "Everything in me is screaming no. This feels wrong at a cellular level."

Through Dream Communication. Your Egbe has been communicating with you your entire life, and dreams are one of its primary channels. If you've been doing the dream work from earlier chapters, you already have information about your agreements. You just need to learn how to interpret it. Before sleep, place your hand on your head and speak: "Egbe, show me what I came here to do. Show me my agreements. Help me understand my path." Then let it go. Write down what comes. Over time, patterns emerge. Your Egbe will show you the same information in multiple ways until you get it.

Through What Life Has Already Required of You. Sometimes the clearest indicator of your agreements is simply looking at what life has already asked you to survive, navigate, master, or transform. The struggles you've already faced reveal what you're meant to teach. If you've navigated divorce and rebuilt your life, you might be here to teach others how to survive endings and create new beginnings. If you've overcome addiction, you might be here to demonstrate that recovery is possible. If you've healed from chronic illness, you might be here to guide others through health challenges. The losses you've experienced often clear space for what you're meant to create. When relationships end, jobs disappear, homes burn down, structures collapse, it feels like destruction. And it is. But destruction creates space. What have you already survived and transformed? That transformed wound is often your qualification to help others facing similar paths.

Common Categories of Soul Agreements

As you explore your agreements, it helps to have some frameworks for understanding what you might be working with. These aren't rigid boxes.

They're mirrors for reflection. Most people have two or three primary agreements with several secondary ones.

Creative Agreements. You came to create. Art, music, writing, film, design, innovation, ideas. Your deepest fulfillment comes from making things that didn't exist before. You're probably restless in purely administrative or execution-focused roles. Your job is to create and share your creations, not hoard them waiting for perfect conditions.

What this looks like in practice: The creative agreement isn't about being famous or successful (though that might happen). It's about EXPRESSING. Your job is to make what wants to be made through you, whether that's a painting, a business, a garden, a meal, a framework, a community, or something entirely new. The world needs what you're here to create. Not because it's perfect, but because it carries your frequency. Create it.

Healing Agreements. You came to facilitate transformation in others, whether through traditional healing modalities, therapy, coaching, energy work, or simply holding space. People have always told you their secrets, asked for your advice, sought your presence during crisis. The healing agreement doesn't mean you have to heal everyone. It means healing is your work, your gift, your contribution.

What this looks like in practice: The healing agreement doesn't mean your life has to be defined by your wounds. It means you transform them into medicine, for yourself first, then for others. You don't have to become a professional healer (though you might). You just have to be willing to do your own healing work and allow what you've learned to serve others.

The wound becomes the gift when you stop hiding it and start offering what it taught you.

Teaching Agreements. You came to transmit knowledge, skills, or wisdom. You naturally break down complex ideas into digestible pieces. You get lit up by watching others learn and grow. Your job is to teach what you know, in whatever form feels natural.

What this looks like in practice: The teaching agreement doesn't require you to stand in front of a classroom (though it might). It means you're here to illuminate what's confusing, to make accessible what feels inaccessible, to help people understand themselves and their world more clearly.

Teach what you know. In whatever form feels natural. Your clarity is needed.

Relational Agreements. Connection is your primary curriculum. Your most significant growth has come through relationship. You are deeply affected by relational dynamics. Your job is to learn relational mastery and demonstrate it: healing attachment wounds, building partnerships you didn't see modeled, creating chosen family.

What this looks like in practice: The relational agreement doesn't mean you're guaranteed easy partnerships. It means relationships are where you do your deepest work: learning how to be seen, how to see others, how to hold boundaries while staying open, how to love without losing yourself.

Service Agreements. There's a mission larger than yourself. A cause, community, or population you are meant to serve. You are pulled toward specific groups or issues. You're willing to sacrifice comfort for impact. Serve what calls you, but do not abandon yourself in the process.

What this looks like in practice: The service agreement doesn't mean martyrdom or self-abandonment. It means there's a mission larger than your personal comfort that you're meant to serve. That might be through your career (nonprofit work, activism, policy change) or through how you use your gifts (pro bono services, volunteer work, community organizing).

Liberation Agreements. You came to break patterns. Generational trauma, cultural conditioning, systemic oppression, limiting beliefs. You consistently refuse to do things "the way they've always been done." Your life looks radically different from your family of origin. Break what needs breaking. Your freedom frees others.

What this looks like in practice: The liberation agreement isn't about rebellion for its own sake. It's about freeing yourself and others from patterns that no longer serve. That might mean breaking generational trauma in your family, leaving a religion that confined you, creating a business model that doesn't exploit, or simply living so authentically that you give others permission to do the same.

Mastery Agreements. You came to develop deep capacity in one specific area: power, surrender, trust, boundaries, voice, discernment. Life keeps giving you opportunities to learn it until you do. The same lesson shows up repeatedly in different forms. You're meant to become a living demonstration of what is possible when that thing is mastered.

What this looks like in practice: The mastery agreement means you're here to learn something so deeply that you become a living demonstration of it. If you're mastering power, you'll be given power and asked not to abuse it. If you're mastering surrender, you'll face situations where control is impossible. If you're mastering voice, you'll be put in positions where speaking up costs you something.

This is hard work. But mastery isn't achieved through ease. It's achieved through repeated encounter with the edge of your capacity, then expanding past it. Do the work. The mastery is the point.

Don't force yourself into a single category. Use these as mirrors for reflection, not boxes for containment. Your agreements are unique to you.

What to Do Once You Know

So you've identified your agreements, through pattern recognition, through divination, through your body's wisdom, through what life has already shown you. Now what?

Knowing your agreements is step one. Living them is the work.

And what you need to understand is this: you don't need perfect clarity to begin.

Most people wait. They think they need to know every detail, see the whole path, have all the answers before they take the first step. But that's not how soul agreements work.

You see the next step. You take it. Then the next step reveals itself. Then you take that one. The path clarifies through walking it, not before.

Start where you are. If you know you have a creative agreement but you're working a job that has nothing to do with your art, don't quit tomorrow and expect your creative work to pay your bills next month. Start by creating consistently. An hour a day, a few hours a week, whatever you can sustain. The agreement isn't "become a professional artist immediately." The agreement is "create." So create.

If you know you have a healing agreement but you're not a trained therapist, don't go back to school for a degree you can't afford. Start by doing your own healing work. Read. Go to therapy. Work with practitioners who've walked the path before you. The agreement isn't "save everyone." The agreement is "heal yourself, then offer what you learned." So start with yourself.

If you know you have a teaching agreement but you don't have a platform or credentials, don't wait until you're "qualified." Start teaching what you know to whoever will listen: friends, family, online communities, local groups. The agreement isn't "become famous." The agreement is "share what you know." So share.

You don't need permission. You don't need perfect conditions. You don't need to be ready.

You just need to start.

Give yourself permission. This is the part most people get stuck on. They know what they're meant to do. They can feel it. Their body confirms it. Their life has been pointing toward it for years. But they're waiting for someone to tell them it is okay. If it won't leave you alone, if your body says yes, if it keeps calling you despite every logical reason to ignore it: that's your agreement. And you have permission to live it. Not from me. Not from your Egbe. From your Enikeji Orun. The only permission that matters.

Expect resistance. Living your agreements will cost you something. Not because the universe is punishing you, but because alignment requires you to release what's misaligned. You might lose relationships with people who preferred the version of you that stayed small and safe. You might lose financial security when you leave the stable job to pursue the risky calling. You might lose your reputation when you speak truths that make people uncomfortable. You might lose your comfort when you choose growth over stagnation. This is normal. This doesn't mean you're on the wrong path. It means you're on the RIGHT path, and everything that doesn't belong there is falling away to make space for what does. Resistance, internal and external, is part of the process. Expect it. Don't let it stop you.

Trust the unfolding. You won't see the whole path. You'll see the next step. Take it. Then you'll see the step after that. Take it. Then circumstances will shift and a door will open you didn't know existed. Walk through it. This is how soul agreements unfold: not through perfect planning, but through trust and movement. Your Egbe orchestrates the path AS you walk it. It can't show you what's five years ahead because you're not ready for that information yet. You're ready for the next step. So take it. Then trust that the step after that will reveal itself when you're ready.

When You Are Still Not Sure

And if you've read this entire chapter and you're still sitting there thinking, "I STILL don't know what my agreements are. I don't see clear patterns. I'm not getting dreams. My body is not giving me obvious signals. I feel lost."

That's okay.

Uncertainty is part of the process for many people. Not everyone gets clear downloads. Not everyone has access to divination. Not everyone can afford Akashic Records readings or Ifa consultations. Not everyone's path is obvious.

If you're in this place, know this: your agreements will reveal themselves through living. You don't have to have it all figured out before you start. You just have to pay attention to what lights you up, what drains you, what won't leave you alone, and what your body says yes or no to. Then move toward the yes. Release the no. And trust that the path will clarify as you walk it.

Start with what's in front of you. If you don't know your grand life purpose, that's fine. What needs your attention right now? What problem can you solve today? What person can you help this week? What small thing can you create? Do that. Your agreements aren't always about massive, world-changing missions. Sometimes they're about showing up with presence and integrity in the small moments.

For some people, the agreement is not to know exactly what they're doing. The agreement is to learn how to trust without certainty, to move without guarantees, to build faith through not-knowing. If that is you, stop fighting it. The uncertainty is not a problem to solve. It's the path itself.

Your Egbe hasn't abandoned you. Just because you cannot see the path clearly doesn't mean your soul group isn't there. It's orchestrating circumstances. It's creating synchronicities. It's supporting you even when you cannot feel it.

Keep showing up. Keep paying attention. Keep choosing what feels true. The clarity will come.

And in the meantime, live. Fully. Honestly. With as much alignment as you can access right now. That's enough. It's always been enough.

From Discovery to Sustainability

You now have the tools for discovering what you came here to do: reading the patterns in your life, accessing information through multiple methods, recognizing common agreement categories, and taking action even before you have perfect clarity.

But knowing your agreements and living them are different things. And living them for a week is different from living them for decades.

The final chapter addresses what nobody tells you about spiritual awakening: it doesn't end. There's no moment where you finally "get it" and coast for the rest of your life in perfect alignment. The work continues. Every day. For the rest of your life.

You've discovered your agreements. Now let's make sure you can live them for the long haul.

REFLECTION QUESTIONS

Before you move forward, take time to sit with these questions:

1. Looking at your entire life as a timeline, what 3-5 themes have been consistent across different phases, relationships, and contexts? What is your life showing you that you are working on?
2. What skill, gift, or capacity do you have that feels so natural you have undervalued it? What if that is exactly what you came here to express?
3. What wound have you experienced that forced you to develop a specific capacity? Who might need what you learned through that struggle?
4. What has been calling you for years that you keep dismissing as impractical, impossible, or "not realistic"? What if that persistent pull is your agreement, asking for your attention?
5. If you knew with absolute certainty that you had full permission to live your agreements starting tomorrow, no external validation needed, what would you begin? What is the very first step?

CHAPTER 12

WALKING FORWARD: LIVING SOUL-ALIGNED IN A WORLD THAT ISN'T

You know what nobody tells you about spiritual awakening?

It doesn't end.

There's no moment where you finally "get it" and coast for the rest of your life in perfect alignment, effortless flow, and unshakeable clarity. There's no graduation ceremony where your Egbe hands you a certificate that says "Congratulations, you figured it out. You're done now."

The work continues. Every day. For the rest of your life.

And here's the other thing nobody tells you: the world you're living in wasn't designed for soul-aligned people.

The systems, structures, and cultural conditioning that surround you were built to reward conformity, productivity, and performance—not authenticity, alignment, or spiritual integrity. You're going to face resistance. From people who don't understand. From systems that punish deviation. From your own conditioning that screams at you to stay small and safe.

This chapter is about how to keep walking when the path gets hard. How to sustain this work when you're tired, doubting, or facing consequences for living your truth. How to stay aligned in a world that constantly asks you to compromise.

Because knowing your agreements is one thing. Living them for decades, through difficulty, without giving up: that's another thing entirely.

This is the chapter about endurance. Sustainability. The long game.

Let's talk about what it actually takes to walk this path for the rest of your life.

The Reality Check: What You're Going to Face

I need to be honest about what living your soul agreements actually looks like. Not to discourage you, but to prepare you.

People Won't Understand

The moment you start living differently (making choices based on soul alignment rather than social acceptability) people will have opinions.

Your family might not understand why you left the stable career they sacrificed so much to help you access. Your friends might not get why you're not available for the same activities you used to participate in. Your partner might struggle with the changes in you as you become more yourself.

Some people will think you're selfish. Some will think you're crazy. Some will think you're going through a phase and you'll "come to your senses" eventually.

This is normal. And it's painful.

You're not imagining their confusion, judgment, or disapproval. It's real. And it's not your job to make them understand. Most of them won't, because they're not living from the same place you are.

Your job is to stay true anyway.

Not to convince them. Not to justify yourself. Not to perform your spiritual journey for their approval.

Just to keep walking your path, knowing that some people will come with you and some won't. And both are okay.

Systems Will Push Back

Most workplaces don't reward soul alignment over productivity. Most industries don't care about your agreements. They care about your output. When you prioritize what's aligned over what's profitable, you may face real consequences: lost income, lost opportunities, labels like "difficult" or "unprofessional."

The education system doesn't teach spiritual sovereignty. The healthcare system doesn't validate body wisdom. The economic system doesn't support people who value meaning over money. You're going to bump up against structures built on different values. Sometimes those structures will punish you for not conforming.

This doesn't mean you did something wrong. It means you're operating from a different paradigm, and the old paradigm doesn't know what to do with you.

Stay aligned anyway. The cost of conformity is higher than the cost of resistance.

Alignment Will Feel Too Costly Sometimes

There will be moments when living your agreements requires sacrificing something precious—a relationship, a job, your security, your reputation. You'll be tempted to choose comfort over truth.

And maybe you will do that. Maybe you'll choose the easier path for a while because you're human and you need a break from the intensity of always choosing soul over safety.

That's allowed. Just be honest about what you're doing. The moment you start lying to yourself about why you're choosing misalignment, you create static that makes it impossible to hear your Egbe.

You Will Doubt Everything

There will be moments when you question whether any of this is real. Whether your Egbe exists or you've been talking to yourself. Whether your agreements are genuine or invented.

Doubt is part of the process. Your Egbe doesn't disappear when you doubt. It's still there, still orchestrating, still supporting. Sometimes the support looks like silence. Sometimes it looks like difficulty. Sometimes it looks like nothing happening at all.

Because not every season is about dramatic transformation. Some seasons are about building capacity through endurance. Some seasons are about learning to trust when you can't see the path. Some seasons are about staying committed when there's no immediate reward.

Those seasons are hard. And doubt is normal. Walk through the doubt. It won't kill you. Your faith will be stronger on the other side.

Your Egbe Will Feel Silent

There will be times when dreams stop, synchronicities disappear, and you get nothing from your practices. This doesn't mean abandonment. It means you're being asked to trust what you already know instead of seeking constant confirmation.

Your Egbe speaks loudest when you need course correction or encouragement for a big leap. When you're walking steadily on your path, doing the work, living your agreements—it doesn't need to shout. You're already doing what you came to do.

The silence is trust. It trusts you to keep walking without external validation. Learn to trust yourself the same way. This is maturity in spiritual relationship: doing the work without needing constant signs. Your Egbe isn't absent. It's giving you room to grow into your own knowing.

None of this means you're on the wrong path. It means you're on the path. The real one. And the real path is hard sometimes.

Walk anyway.

Sustainability Over Intensity

One of the biggest mistakes people make when they discover their soul agreements is they try to overhaul their entire life overnight.

They quit their job without a plan. They end all their relationships in one dramatic purge. They move across the country on impulse. They burn their life down and expect their Egbe to catch them.

Sometimes that works. Sometimes dramatic upheaval is exactly what's needed to break free from structures that were suffocating your soul.

But most of the time? That level of intensity isn't sustainable. And after the dramatic gesture, you're left standing in the rubble of your life, exhausted, broke, and wondering why alignment feels so hard.

Living your agreements isn't about intensity. It's about sustainability.

It's not about how fast you can transform. It's about how long you can keep walking without burning out.

Small Daily Choices Compound Over Time

You don't have to blow up your entire life to live your agreements. You just have to make one aligned choice. Then another. Then another.

Choose the aligned thing for breakfast. Then for the conversation you're about to have. Then for the work you do this afternoon. Then for how you spend your evening.

Each choice is small. Each choice feels insignificant in the moment. But choices compound.

Choose alignment 60% of the time, and your life starts shifting. Choose it 70% of the time, and the shift accelerates. Choose it 80% of the time, and your life becomes unrecognizable from what it was five years ago.

You don't need perfection. You need consistency.

Ask yourself every day: "What's one aligned choice I can make today that moves me closer to my agreements?"

Then make it. Then make another one tomorrow.

Over months, over years, those small choices add up to a completely different life.

Build Systems That Support Alignment, Not Just Willpower

Willpower is finite. You can't rely on it to keep you aligned long-term. You need systems: structures, routines, environments, and relationships that make alignment easier than misalignment.

What does this look like practically?

If your agreement involves creativity, build a system that protects your creative time. Block it on your calendar. Treat it as non-negotiable. Create a space in your home where you do your creative work. Eliminate the friction that makes it hard to start.

If your agreement involves healing work, build a system that keeps you resourced. Regular therapy. Bodywork. Community. Practices that help you process what you're holding for others. You can't pour from an empty cup, so make sure the cup-filling is systematic, not just something you do when you're desperate.

If your agreement involves teaching, build a system that allows you to share consistently. A newsletter. A regular gathering. A social media presence. Something that creates rhythm and accountability so you don't just teach when you feel like it.

The system removes the need for constant decision-making. You don't have to wake up every day and decide whether to honor your agreements. The system already decided for you. You just follow it.

This is how you sustain the work long-term. Not through heroic effort, but through intelligent design.

Create Community With People Who Get It

You can't do this alone.

You need people who understand what you're doing, why you're doing it, and what it costs. People who won't judge you for choosing soul over safety. People who celebrate your alignment instead of questioning it.

This might be a spiritual community. It might be a mastermind. It might be a small group of friends who are also walking non-traditional paths. It might be online communities where you've found your people.

Wherever you find them, cultivate those relationships. Show up for them. Let them show up for you. Share your struggles. Celebrate your breakthroughs. Normalize the difficulty so you don't feel like you're the only one facing resistance.

Community reminds you that you're not crazy. Other people are choosing this path too. Other people are facing the same challenges. Other people are staying committed even when it's hard.

You're not alone. But you have to intentionally build connection with people who remind you of that.

Give Yourself Permission to Rest, Doubt, and Stumble

This is lifelong work. You're going to have seasons where you're on fire, aligned, clear, and moving forward with momentum. And you're going to have seasons where you're exhausted, confused, doubting, and barely holding on.

Both are normal. Both are part of the process.

You don't have to be "on" all the time. You don't have to perform spiritual alignment for anyone. You're allowed to be tired. You're allowed to not know. You're allowed to take breaks.

Rest isn't misalignment. Rest is wisdom. Your body, your soul, your Egbe—all of them know you need rest to sustain this work.

So rest. Without guilt. Without shame. Without the story that resting means you're failing.

Rest so you can keep walking for the rest of your life.

When You Drift Off-Path (Because You Will)

Let's address what nobody wants to talk about: **you will drift off-path. Multiple times.**

Not because you're weak or uncommitted. But because you're human, and humans drift. We get tired. We get scared. We get seduced by comfort or approval or security. We make choices we know aren't aligned because in the moment, the misaligned thing feels easier.

This is normal. This doesn't mean you've failed. It means you're learning.

But you need to know how to come back. Because drifting off-path isn't the problem. Staying off-path is.

Notice the Signs

Your body will tell you when you're off-path, usually before your mind catches up.

The signs look like:

- Chronic fatigue that rest doesn't fix
- Illness or injury that doesn't make medical sense
- Depression or anxiety that seems to come out of nowhere
- Friction in relationships that used to be smooth

- Loss or endings that feel chaotic or sudden
- Opportunities disappearing or doors repeatedly closing
- A sense of flatness where nothing feels meaningful anymore

These aren't random. These are your Egbe, your Enikeji Orun, your body, all trying to tell you that something is off. You're living out of alignment, and the consequences are showing up in your physical, emotional, and relational life.

Don't ignore the signs. They're precision guidance.

When you notice them, pause. Don't spiral into shame or panic. Just notice: "Oh. I've drifted. Something is off."

That awareness is the first step back.

Don't Shame Yourself—Course-Correct

The fastest way to stay stuck off-path is to shame yourself for being there.

"I should have known better. I'm a spiritual teacher, and I'm still making these mistakes. What's wrong with me? Why can't I get this right?"

Stop. That's ego talking, not soul. And ego will keep you stuck in shame instead of helping you move toward correction.

Your Egbe doesn't shame you for drifting. It just waits for you to notice and come back. It's seen you drift before. It''ll see you drift again. It's not disappointed. It's patient.

You need to be patient with yourself too.

When you notice you're off-path, the question isn't "What's wrong with me?" The question is "What needs to change?"

Skip the self-flagellation. Move straight to course-correction.

Ask: "What Am I Avoiding?" and Tell the Truth

Most of the time when you drift off-path, it's because you're avoiding something your soul is asking you to face.

A difficult conversation. A necessary ending. A big leap. A truth you don't want to acknowledge. A wound you don't want to heal.

So you distract yourself. You stay busy. You choose comfort. You numb out. You perform productivity while avoiding the actual work your soul needs you to do.

And slowly, imperceptibly, you drift.

When you realize you're off-path, ask yourself: **"What have I been avoiding?"**

Then tell the truth. Out loud if possible. Write it down if that helps. But name it.

"I've been avoiding the conversation with my partner about our relationship."

"I've been avoiding starting my business because I'm terrified of failure."

"I've been avoiding grief by staying perpetually busy."

"I've been avoiding my body's need for rest because I've attached my worth to productivity."

The avoidance is the problem. And you can't solve a problem you won't name.

So name it. Then do the thing you've been avoiding. Not perfectly. Not all at once. Just take one step toward it.

Have the conversation. Start the business, even if it's just registering the LLC. Let yourself feel the grief for ten minutes. Rest for one day.

The moment you stop avoiding and start facing what needs to be faced, the path clarifies. Your Egbe can work with you again. The signs shift from friction to flow.

But you have to tell the truth first.

Make One Aligned Choice, Then Another

You don't have to fix everything at once. You just have to make one choice that brings you back toward alignment.

Then make another one. Then another.

If you've been off-path for months, one choice won't magically put you back on track. But it will shift the direction. And the next choice will shift it a little more. And eventually, the small course-corrections add up to being back on your path.

Don't overwhelm yourself trying to overhaul everything immediately. Just make the next aligned choice. That's all you need to do.

Trust Your Egbe Is Still There, Waiting

When you drift, your Egbe doesn't leave. It doesn't withdraw its support. It doesn't judge you for being human.

It just waits. It creates friction to wake you up. It orchestrates circumstances that make misalignment increasingly uncomfortable. It holds the memory of your agreements while you temporarily forget them.

And when you come back, when you notice you've drifted and you start course-correcting, it meets you there. Immediately.

The relationship doesn't need to be rebuilt. It was never broken. You just stopped listening for a while. And now you're listening again.

So trust that it's still there. It always has been. It always will be.

And come back. It's waiting.

The Ripple Effect: Why Your Alignment Matters Beyond You

Here's something that might surprise you: your soul alignment isn't just about you.

Yes, you made agreements before birth. Yes, you came here to live them. Yes, your Egbe supports you, your Enikeji Orun guides you, and your Ori chose this path.

But your alignment ripples out in ways you can't fully measure.

You Give Others Permission

Every time you choose alignment over conformity, you give someone else permission to do the same.

When you leave the job that was draining you, someone watching notices that it's possible to choose differently.

When you end the relationship that wasn't serving you, someone in your life sees that they don't have to stay in misalignment just because they committed to something that's no longer right.

When you start the creative work you've been hiding, someone else gets permission to share their art too.

When you speak the truth that costs you approval, someone else learns that honesty is more valuable than being liked.

You don't have to announce what you're doing or perform your journey publicly. Just by living differently, you shift what's possible for the people around you.

Your alignment gives others permission to align. Even when you don't know they're watching.

You Heal Your Lineage Backward and Forward

When you break patterns that have been running through your family for generations (addiction, abuse, scarcity, silence, shame) you don't just heal yourself. You heal the lineage.

Your ancestors carry the wounds they couldn't heal in their lifetimes. They pass them down, hoping someone in the line will have the capacity, resources, and awareness to transform them.

When you do that work, you heal backward. You release your ancestors from patterns they couldn't break. You complete what they started.

And you heal forward. The children who come after you (your biological children or the next generation in your community) won't inherit the same wounds. You broke the transmission. They get to start from a different foundation.

This is collective healing. It doesn't just benefit you. It benefits everyone connected to you through blood, through soul group, through the energetic web of ancestry.

Your healing is never just personal. It's ancestral. It's generational. It's part of the larger work of consciousness evolving through time.

You Shift the Collective Field

Every time you choose truth over performance, alignment over approval, soul over safety—you shift the field.

Consciousness is interconnected. What you do here affects the whole. When you live your agreements, you raise the frequency of the collective field. You make it easier for the next person to choose alignment because you've already walked that path and created an energetic blueprint they can follow.

This is why your work matters even when it feels small. Even when you're just living your life, making aligned choices, doing your creative work, healing your wounds, using your gifts—you're contributing to the evolution of collective consciousness.

You're not separate from the whole. You're a node in the web. And when you align, the entire web shifts.

You might never know who you've impacted. You might never see the ripple effects of your choices. But they're there.

Your alignment matters. Not just for you. For all of us.

You Become the Bridge You're Meant to Be

Remember Chapter 9? You are the bridge between Orun and Aiye. You are Egbe expressing in form. You are Enikeji Orun experiencing density. You are consciousness meeting itself.

When you live your agreements, you embody that truth. You demonstrate what it looks like when the unseen becomes seen, when spiritual principles translate into physical action, when soul agreements express through human choices.

You become living proof that it's possible to live soul-aligned in a world that wasn't designed for it.

And that matters. Because people need to see it's possible before they'll try it themselves.

You're not just walking your path for you. You're walking it for everyone who comes after you, everyone who's watching from the sidelines wondering if they could do it too, everyone who needs to see someone living differently before they believe it's an option.

You are the bridge. And every time you choose alignment, you strengthen that bridge for everyone else who needs to cross it.

That's the ripple effect. That's why your work matters beyond your personal evolution.

You're not doing this alone. And you're not doing it just for yourself.

The Invitation Forward

So here we are. You know the cosmology. You've seen what embodied alignment looks like. You have practices for building relationship with your soul group. You know how to discover and live your agreements.

Now you just have to do it.

This isn't a one-time revelation. This is a lifelong practice.

Every day, you'll face the same choice: alignment or performance. Truth or comfort. Soul or safety. Your agreements or someone else's expectations. Every day, you'll have opportunities to drift. And every day, you'll have opportunities to come back.

That's the work. Not perfection. Not enlightenment. Just choosing alignment, again and again.

Live what you know. Your body tells the truth, listen to it. Your gifts are agreements to use them, use them. The pull that won't leave you alone is your path, follow it.

Trust what you feel. Not what others tell you to feel. Not what makes logical sense. What you actually feel in your body when you get quiet and ask the truth. That's your Enikeji Orun speaking.

Honor what calls you. The creative work. The difficult conversation. The necessary ending. The terrifying beginning. Whatever won't leave you alone—that's your agreement.

Release what drains you. The relationships requiring you to shrink. The work that depletes your soul. The beliefs keeping you small. Let them go with honesty, not drama. Make space for what actually belongs.

Speak your truth. Even when it costs you. Even when it's inconvenient. Your voice is part of your agreement.

Use your gifts. Whatever energizes you instead of depleting you. That's what you brought into this incarnation to express. Not someday. Now.

Walk your path. The one your soul chose. The one your Ori picked at Àjàlá's house. Even when it's lonely. Even when it's costly. Even when you can't see where it's going.

Your Egbe will meet you in every step. It always has. It always will.

The Final Truth

When this gets hard (and it will get hard), remember this:

You're not doing this to achieve some spiritual ideal. You're not trying to transcend your humanity or become perfectly aligned or never struggle again.

You're doing this because you made agreements before you were born, and honoring those agreements is the most meaningful way you can spend your time here.

You're doing this because living in alignment feels like coming home, even when it's difficult.

You're doing this because the alternative (performing someone else's life, hiding your gifts, ignoring your knowing, shrinking to fit spaces too small for your soul) that alternative kills you slowly. And you've already tried that. It doesn't work.

You're doing this because your soul won't let you do anything else.

Once you know, you can't unknow. Once you've felt what alignment feels like, you can't go back to pretending misalignment is fine. Once you've recognized your Egbe, heard your Enikeji Orun, lived your agreements even for a moment, you can't forget.

You might drift. You might resist. You might choose comfort over truth for a season.

But you'll come back. Because your soul won't let you stay away.

That's not a burden. That's a gift. Your soul loves you too much to let you waste this incarnation living someone else's path.

So trust that. Trust that even when you drift, you'll come back. Trust that your Egbe is patient. Trust that your agreements are strong enough to pull you home, again and again, for the rest of your life.

And trust that you're exactly where you need to be.

Right now. In this moment. With all your clarity and all your confusion. With all your alignment and all your resistance. With all your breakthroughs and all your struggles.

You're exactly where you need to be.

Not because everything is perfect. But because this—right here, right now, exactly as it is—this is your path. This is what your Ori chose. This is what your Egbe is supporting. This is what your Enikeji Orun is experiencing.

You're not behind. You're not failing. You're not doing it wrong.

You're walking. And the walking is the point.

So keep walking.

Your Egbe is with you. It has been with you through every lifetime, every version of you, every struggle and every triumph. It witnessed the moment you chose this incarnation. It knows what you came to do. And it's celebrating every moment you choose to remember.

You're not alone.

You never have been.

You are Egbe Orun, walking in Aiye, living your agreements, becoming the bridge you came here to be.

Now walk accordingly.

CLOSING REFLECTION

Take a moment. Put your hand on your chest or your head. Breathe. Connect with your Ori. Connect with your Enikeji Orun. Connect with your Egbe.

And ask yourself:

"What is one aligned choice I can make today that honors the agreements I came here to live?"

Then make it.

Not tomorrow. Not when you're ready. Not when conditions are perfect.

Today. Now. This moment.

Make one aligned choice.

Then tomorrow, make another.

And the next day, another.

That's how you live your agreements. That's how you walk your path. That's how you become the bridge.

One choice at a time. For the rest of your life.

Your Egbe is waiting.

Walk.

BUILDING DAILY PRACTICE WITH YOUR SOUL GROUP

You don't need elaborate ceremony to work with your Egbe. You don't need initiation, a priestess, or special tools. You need presence, consistency, and the willingness to listen.

Throughout this book, you've learned what Egbe is, how it orchestrates your life, and what kind of relationship this actually is. In Chapter 5, you learned to recognize the orchestration that's already happening, to notice synchronicities, trust your body, pay attention to dreams, and create space to listen.

This chapter gives you practices for actively building the relationship. These aren't recognition practices (that's Chapter 5). These are cultivation practices, ways to show up consistently that strengthen your connection and make you more receptive to guidance over time.

Think of these as relationship-building practices, not rituals to get what you want. Your Egbe isn't a vending machine. It's your soul family, the collective consciousness you're part of. The goal isn't to manipulate it into giving you things. The goal is to remember who you are and live accordingly.

The Foundation: Daily Acknowledgment

The simplest practice is also the most powerful: acknowledge your Egbe daily.

This doesn't require elaborate language or formal prayer. It can be as simple as:

"Egbe mi o, I greet you. Thank you for walking with me."

Say it in the morning when you wake up. Say it at night before sleep. Say it when something synchronistic happens that makes you think, "That wasn't random."

What you're doing is training your awareness to recognize that you're not alone. You're not navigating life as a disconnected individual trying to figure everything out by yourself. You have a collective consciousness actively supporting you, orchestrating circumstances, creating opportunities.

Acknowledgment builds the relationship. It strengthens the connection. It makes you more receptive to the guidance that's already there.

I do this every morning before I get out of bed. Three breaths. Then: *"Egbe mo pe o. Egbe mo pe o. Egbe mo pe o. Thank you for another day. Show me what I need to see."*

That's it. Twenty seconds. But it shifts how I move through my entire day.

Practice One: The Morning Alignment Check

Before you check your phone, before you make coffee, before you do anything else:

Sit quietly for three to five minutes. Place your hand on your heart or your belly. Ask:

"What does my soul need today? What did I agree to do that I'm avoiding? Where am I forcing something that isn't mine?"

Then listen. Not with your thinking mind, but with your body, your gut, your inner knowing.

You might get words. You might get images. You might just get a feeling of "yes, this" or "no, not that."

Whatever comes, trust it. Write it down if that helps you remember.

This practice isn't about getting elaborate downloads from the spirit realm. It's about tuning into what you already know at the soul level before your day pulls you into reaction mode.

Some mornings I get clear guidance: "Cancel that meeting, it's not aligned." Other mornings I just get a sense of peace, a feeling of "you're on track, keep going." Both matter.

Practice Two: Feeding Your Egbe (Traditional Offering)

In traditional Yoruba practice, you feed your Egbe through offerings. This isn't superstition. It's energetic exchange, reciprocity, acknowledgment of relationship.

If you're initiated into Egbe or work with a traditional priest, you'll have specific instructions for offerings based on your particular Egbe class. Follow those instructions.

If you're not initiated but feel called to make offerings, here's a simple, universal approach:

What you'll need: A glass of clean water, a white plate or cloth, a food offering (traditional options: sugar cane, honey, fruits, sweets, kola nut)

The Practice:

Create a clean space: a small table, a shelf, a corner of your room. This becomes your Egbe space.

Place the white cloth or plate down in the corner.

Set out the offering and the glass of water.

Speak to your Egbe. You can use formal prayer if you know it, or speak from your heart:

"Egbe Aiye. Egbe Orun. I honor you. I acknowledge the agreements we made. Thank you for orchestrating my path. Thank you for the synchronicities, the closed doors, the people you've put in my path. I offer this (name the offering) and water as acknowledgment of our relationship. Continue to guide me. Continue to support me. Help me remember what I came here to do."

Leave the offering for at least a few hours (traditionally twenty-four hours or until the next morning). Then dispose of it respectfully, outside in nature if possible, or wrap it in white cloth and place it in the trash.

Important: Offerings are not bribes. You're not paying your Egbe to give you what you want. You're acknowledging relationship, expressing gratitude, maintaining energetic reciprocity. Never offer meat or alcohol unless specifically instructed through divination with a traditional priest. Different Egbe classes have different taboos.

Practice Three: Egbe Journaling

Your Egbe communicates constantly. Most of the time, we're too busy to notice. Journaling creates space to recognize the patterns, the synchronicities, the orchestration that's already happening.

Daily Egbe Journal Prompts:

Synchronicity Tracking: "What synchronicity happened today? Who showed up unexpectedly? What door closed? What opportunity appeared? How might my Egbe be orchestrating this?"

Resistance Tracking: "Where did I feel resistance today? What am I avoiding? What keeps coming up that I keep dismissing? Is this fear or is this my soul saying 'not yours'?"

Alignment Tracking: "When did I feel most alive today? What was I doing when time disappeared? What felt like breathing instead of straining? Is this what I agreed to do?"

Write for five to ten minutes. Don't edit, don't make it pretty, don't perform. Just notice.

Over time, patterns emerge. You'll see that certain types of synchronicities always precede specific opportunities. You'll notice that your resistance isn't random, it shows up around the exact things your soul agreed to do. You'll recognize that the moments when you feel most alive aren't accidents. They're confirmation that you're aligned.

I have over seven years of journals. When I read back through them, I can see my soul group's orchestration so clearly. Doors that seemed closed at the time were protecting me from paths I was never meant to walk.

Practice Four: Dream Work with Egbe

Your Egbe speaks through dreams. When your conscious mind is quiet, when your ego is offline, when your thinking brain can't interfere, that's when your soul group can communicate clearly.

Before Sleep Practice:

As you're falling asleep, speak to your Egbe (silently or aloud): *"Egbe mi, speak to me tonight. Show me what I need to see. Help me remember what I agreed to do. I'm listening."*

Keep a journal and pen next to your bed.

When you wake, before you move, before you check your phone, before you do anything, lie still and notice what you remember. Images, feelings, symbols, conversations.

Write down whatever you remember, even if it doesn't make sense. Even fragments. The act of recording trains your brain to hold onto the messages.

Soul Group Dreams Often Include:

Recurring dreams: Your Egbe is trying to show you something you keep missing

Dreams about people you haven't thought about in years: Often soul family checking in, reminding you of agreements you made together

Dreams where you "just know" things: Direct download from your Enikeji Orun

Dreams about places you've never been but feel familiar: Possible past-life memories, or your soul showing you where you're headed next

I've received some of my clearest Egbe guidance through dreams. I always experience the dreams from the same perspective. That's how I've learned to distinguish my Egbe dreams from other forms of spirit dream communication.

Practice Five: Walking Meditation with Egbe

Movement can be prayer. Walking can be ceremony.

Go for a walk (in nature if possible, but anywhere works).

As you walk, speak to your Egbe (silently or aloud if you're alone): *"Walk with me. Show me what I need to see. Help me hear what I need to hear."*

Then stop talking. Just walk. Notice what you notice. What thoughts arise. What memories surface. What songs get stuck in your head (sometimes your Egbe communicates through music). What you see that catches your attention. What body sensations arise.

When you get home, write down anything that felt significant. You can also use a voice recorder and record anything that comes to you during your walk.

This isn't about forcing mystical experiences. It's about creating spaciousness where your soul can speak.

Some of my biggest breakthroughs have happened on walks. The solution to a problem I'd been forcing suddenly becomes obvious. A relationship dynamic I couldn't see clearly suddenly makes sense. A decision I'd been agonizing over suddenly feels clear.

Practice Six: Gratitude as Recognition

Gratitude isn't toxic positivity. It's recognition of what's already working.

Your Egbe has been orchestrating circumstances, creating synchronicities, opening doors, closing doors, putting people in your path since before you were born. Most of it you haven't noticed because you've been too busy focusing on what's wrong.

Daily Gratitude Practice:

Every night before sleep, name three things your Egbe orchestrated that day.

Not generic gratitude like "I'm grateful for sunshine." Specific recognition of orchestration:

"Thank you for the email that came exactly when I needed that information."

"Thank you for the traffic that made me late, which meant I avoided the accident I would have been in."

"Thank you for the person who canceled plans, which gave me the space I actually needed."

When you practice gratitude as recognition of orchestration, you train your awareness to see how supported you actually are.

Gratitude builds trust. Trust makes you more receptive to guidance. Receptivity strengthens the relationship.

Practice Seven: Asking for Signs

Your Egbe will communicate through signs, but you have to ask and then actually pay attention.

How to Ask:

Get specific about what you're asking. Not "Should I take this job?" but "If this job aligns with my soul agreements, show me [specific sign]."

Choose a sign that would be unusual enough to notice but possible enough to actually happen. Not "show me a purple elephant" but "show me a hummingbird" or "let me hear this specific song" or "let someone mention this specific concept."

Set a timeframe. "Show me within three days."

Then let it go. Don't obsess, don't hunt for the sign, don't force it. Trust.

Pay attention. The sign often shows up in unexpected ways.

Important: Your Egbe won't always give you the sign you asked for if the answer is "no, this isn't aligned." Silence is also an answer. No sign within your timeframe often means "not this, not now."

What Not to Do: Avoiding Spiritual Dependency

As you build relationship with your Egbe, watch out for these patterns:

Don't abdicate your power. Your Egbe supports you, but it doesn't make your decisions for you. If you're asking it what to have for breakfast, you've gone too far. It's not here to micromanage your life. It's here to support your soul agreements.

Don't blame it when things go wrong. "My Egbe led me here and now it's a mess" is spiritual bypassing. Your Egbe orchestrates circumstances aligned with your agreements. If it's hard, it might be exactly what you chose. Take responsibility.

Don't use it as an excuse to avoid practical action. Your Egbe works through the physical realm. If you need therapy, get therapy. If you need medicine, take medicine. If you need to have a hard conversation, have it. Don't spiritualize away what needs practical action.

Don't become dependent on constant signs and validation. Your Egbe communicates, but you also have inner knowing, discernment, and sovereignty. If you can't make any decision without checking for signs, you're giving away your power.

The goal is collaboration, not dependency. Partnership, not powerlessness.

Building Your Own Practice

These seven practices are starting points, not rigid rules.

You might use all of them. You might use one. You might create your own entirely different approach based on what resonates with your soul.

The only requirement is consistency and honesty.

Your Egbe doesn't need elaborate ceremony. It needs your presence. Your willingness to listen. Your commitment to living what you agreed to do.

Don't try to do all seven practices every day. You'll burn out. Choose one or two that resonate most. Do them consistently for thirty days. Notice what shifts. Then add another practice if you want. Or stay with the ones that work.

The goal isn't to have the most impressive spiritual practice. The goal is to stay in conscious relationship with your soul group while living your actual life.

When You Don't Feel Anything

Some people start these practices and immediately feel connection, receive clear guidance, experience obvious synchronicities.

Others feel nothing.

If you're in the second category, keep going anyway.

Your Egbe doesn't always communicate in ways your conscious mind recognizes. Sometimes the guidance shows up as a sudden clarity about a decision you've been avoiding, a conversation with a friend where they say exactly what you needed to hear, a book falling off a shelf that contains the exact answer you needed, a dream you don't consciously remember but wake up knowing what to do.

Not everyone has dramatic spiritual experiences. That doesn't mean your Egbe isn't working.

I went months doing daily practices before I felt anything I could clearly identify as "Egbe communication." But looking back, I can see it was communicating the whole time. I just didn't have the awareness yet to recognize it.

Trust the process even when you can't feel the results. The relationship is building whether you feel it or not.

The Practice Is the Path

The practices that last aren't the most elaborate. They're the ones you can actually maintain.

Start small. Stay consistent. Trust the orchestration.

Your Egbe doesn't need you to be a spiritual overachiever. It needs you to remember who you are and live accordingly.

That's the practice.

REFLECTION QUESTIONS

Before you move forward, take time to sit with these questions:

1. Which of these seven practices resonates most with you right now? Why?
2. What's your biggest resistance to building daily practice with your Egbe? Is it time, skepticism, fear, or something else?
3. What signs of Egbe orchestration have you already been experiencing but dismissing as coincidence?
4. If you acknowledged your Egbe every morning for thirty days, what do you think would shift?
5. Where are you at risk of spiritual dependency vs. spiritual collaboration? How can you build relationship while maintaining your sovereignty?

APPENDICES

APPENDIX A

Prayers and Invocations for Egbe Connection

Note on Yoruba Orthography: The Yoruba prayers presented here follow standard orthographic conventions found in published Egbe literature. Yoruba pronunciation depends on tonal markers and specific vowel sounds; consult the Pronunciation Key in the Glossary for guidance. Traditional prayers and ese Ifa (verses from the sacred Ifa corpus) are presented in Yoruba with English translations. Some prayers reference the scholarship of Ayo Salami (*Egbe: The Heavenly Mates of Every Human*) and Ifayemisi Elebuibon (*Egbe Orun: Comrades of Heaven*), whose work has been instrumental in preserving and transmitting Egbe knowledge.

The following prayers and invocations can be used for personal practice. They range from traditional Yoruba prayers drawn from the Ifa corpus to contemporary invocations I have developed through my own practice. This appendix is organized into three sections: Traditional Prayers from Odu Ifa, Oriki (Praise Poetry), and Contemporary Prayers for daily use.

Traditional Prayer

Ẹsẹ̀ Ifá from Odù Ifá Ogbè Wẹ̀yìn (Yorùbá)

Ìkí ni, ní Ìjẹ́ ni

Ìjẹ́ ni, ní Ìkí ni

O kú owó ni Ìkí Ọ̀yọ́

Mọnja ni Kétu ń kí ara wọn

Àyọ̀nù ni ti àwọn Ègún

Ẹ̀kan ṣoṣo ni ìkí àgbẹ̀

Bí o bá kí àgbẹ̀ lẹ́ẹ̀mejì

Yó dà bí ẹni pé wọ́n ń tọrọ isu lọ́wọ́ rẹ̀

Bẹ́ẹ̀ ni a ò lè ṣe

Ká mọ̀ mọ́ bí a ṣe ń kí ènìyàn

Adífá fún Fápóhùndà Ayé

Àbúfún Fápóhùndà Òde Ọ̀run

Ẹgbẹ́ ẹ mọ́ mọ́ jẹ́ kí n tẹ́ ọ

Ènìyàn rere kì í tẹ́ bọ̀rọ̀ bọ̀rọ̀

~

English Translation

Greeting has its order, and each land has its way.

Ìjẹ́ has its greeting, and greeting remains greeting.

In Ọ̀yọ́ they greet with 'Ẹ kú owó.'

In Kétu they greet one another with 'Mọnja.'

Among the ancestors, the greeting is joy.

The farmer has only one proper greeting.

If you greet the farmer twice,

it appears as though you are begging him for yams.

That is not the proper way.

One must know how to greet with wisdom and restraint.

Ifá divined for Fápóhùndà on Earth,

and sacrifice was prescribed for Fápóhùndà in the spirit realm.

'Ẹgbẹ́, know me well and allow me to step safely,' he prayed.

A good person does not walk carelessly through life.

~

REFLECTIONS

This verse teaches that destiny unfolds through proper relationship, restraint, and remembrance. Every realm has its protocol, and every blessing has an agreement attached to it. Ẹgbẹ́ is not sustained by noise, entitlement, or neglect, but by balance, humility, and fulfilled promises. Excess familiarity breeds loss of respect, and silence where offering is required leads to spiritual withdrawal. A person who walks gently, honors agreements, and remembers the unseen partners of their destiny will never walk alone. Those who forget where their support comes from may still rise for a time, but their ground will not hold.

Source: Odù Ifá Ogbè Wẹ̀yìn.

Traditional Egbe Invocation (Yoruba)

This is a traditional praise and invocation used to call upon Egbe.

In Yoruba:

Ẹgbẹ́ ọga ọ̀gọ́
Alábẹ̀lẹ́nù a ń sàsí
Àtẹ́lẹsìn tẹ̀lẹ́
A pọ̀ jọjọ bí erùpẹ̀
Bọ̀rọ̀kìní òde Òrun tí kì jẹ́ kí ti ayé ó tẹ̀
Ẹ wá gba wa
Ẹ má jẹ́ kí a tẹ̀

Translation:

Heavenly mates, the great ones
You with umbrella under which people seek solace
You who walk with the prosperous
You are plentiful like sand
Heavenly dignitaries who prevent those on earth from falling into disgrace
Come to our aid
Do not let us be disgraced

Traditional Prayer from Odu Ifa Osa Meji

This is a traditional prayer that speaks to the relationship between Egbe in Orun and their counterparts in Aiye.

In Yoruba:

Ìsànsá méjì ní kí ara wọn jéjéjé
A dífá fún Ẹgbẹ́ Ọ̀run, a bù fún ti Aiyé
Bọ̀rọ̀kìní Ọ̀run ẹ má jẹ́ kí ti Ayé ó tẹ̀
Bọ̀rọ̀kìní Ọ̀run ẹ gba wa
Tí Ayé ń tẹ̀ lọ

Translation:

It is the two companions who greet each other gently
Divination was cast for Egbe of Heaven, and also for those of Earth
Heavenly dignitaries, do not allow those on earth to be disgraced
Heavenly dignitaries, come to our aid
Those on earth are about to face difficulty

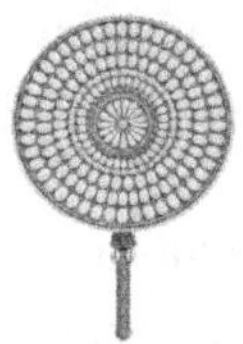

The Story of Fápóhùndà and His Ẹgbẹ́ (A narrative from the Ifa oral tradition)

One day, while Fápóhùndà was still in the spirit realm, he lived closely with his Ẹgbẹ́. He had a deep connection with them. They met often and discussed matters concerning both heaven and earth. Their relationship was strong, grounded in trust, shared purpose, and mutual understanding.

When the time came for Fápóhùndà to make his sojourn to the Earth, he went before his Ẹgbẹ́ and spoke to them openly. He asked for their support as he descended into the world, praying that his life on Earth would be successful and meaningful. His Ẹgbẹ́ agreed without hesitation and promised to stand behind him.

Before leaving, Fápóhùndà made a clear vow. He promised that whatever abundance, wealth, or success he received on Earth, he would remember his Ẹgbẹ́ and send offerings back to them in gratitude and acknowledgment of their support.

When he arrived on Earth, his life flourished. He married, had children, and his household expanded rapidly. His compound grew into a prosperous estate. He had farm animals, abundant crops, and every visible sign of wealth and stability. His name became associated with success and growth.

However, as his prosperity increased, Fápóhùndà slowly forgot his promise. He no longer remembered his Ẹgbẹ́, nor did he send offerings as he had vowed. He celebrated, hosted gatherings, and enjoyed the fruits of his success, but the spiritual relationship that made it all possible was neglected.

One morning, he woke up to devastation. His farm animals were dead. His crops were withering. The wealth that had once flowed steadily into his life began to dry up. Confused and distressed, Fápóhùndà could not understand what had gone wrong.

He consulted an Ifá priest, who performed divination. Ogbè Wèyìn appeared. The message was clear. His Ẹgbẹ́ was deeply upset. He had broken a sacred agreement. Though embarrassed, Fápóhùndà knew the truth. He had failed to honor his word.

The priest instructed him to offer a sheep and to host a proper spiritual feast for his Ẹgbẹ́ in the spirit realm, restoring balance and respect between them. Only then could their support return.

Fápóhùndà complied fully. He performed the sacrifice, renewed his commitment, and remembered his Ẹgbẹ́ as he had promised. Slowly, life returned to balance. His crops grew again. His animals multiplied. Prosperity returned to his household.

From that time forward, Fápóhùndà understood that success without remembrance is temporary. By honoring his Ẹgbẹ́ and keeping his word, he restored the sacred connection that allowed abundance to flow freely between heaven and earth.

Òrìṣà Song

Written by Dr. La Toya Davis, Iya Egbenike
Song Available on Music Streaming Platforms

EGBE WALK WITH ME (2025)

Egbe Orun, I remember you

Egbe Orun, I honor you

Egbe mi, heavenly friends

Walk with me, walk with me

Before I took breath, before I saw light

I sat in Orun, choosing this life

You knew my purpose, you knew my name

You knew the fire I would carry in my veins

You said, "When you forget, we will remind you"

"You will not be alone, we will stand behind you"

Every step I take on this earthly ground

I feel your presence when my heart hears that sound

When the road feels heavy and I do not see

You arrange the signs that guide my feet

From the unseen realms you speak so clear

Egbe Orun, I know you are near

Egbe, walk with me, walk with me

Heavenly comrades, surround me

From Orun to Aiye, I am never alone

I hear your song, it calls me home

Egbe, dance with me, dance with me

Lift my spirit, set me free

Every blessing that flows to me

Is a praise song for our destiny

You move through my dreams, through the ones that I meet

In the books that find me, in the people I greet

You open paths that I could not see

You close the doors that are not for me

When I want to quit, you rise like a wave

Whispering softly, "Beloved, be brave"

You send me courage, you send me light

You help my spirit remember its might

When the world feels loud and my heart feels small

You remind me I am part of it all

From the star-filled sky to the ocean floor

Egbe Orun, I hear you once more

Egbe, walk with me, walk with me

Heavenly comrades, surround me

From Orun to Aiye, I am never alone

I hear your song, it calls me home

Egbe, dance with me, dance with me

Lift my spirit, set me free

Every blessing that flows to me

Is a praise song for our destiny

Egbe mi, mo yin yin, I praise you

All my days, I will not forget you

In my joy, in my tears, you are near

In my courage, in my fears, you are here

Iyalode Egbe, hear my voice

Bless my path, bless my choice

Let my life shine bright and true

So the world can see your light come through

Call: Egbe Orun, mo ki yin o

Response: Mo ki yin, mo ki yin, mo ki yin o

Call: Comrades of heaven, stand by me

Response: Stand by me, stand by me, stand by me

Call: When I rise, let us rise as one

Call: As in Orun, so in Aiye

Response: So in Aiye, so in Aiye

Egbe, walk with me, walk with me

Heavenly comrades, surround me

From Orun to Aiye , I am never alone

I hear your song, it calls me home

Egbe, dance with me, dance with me

Lift my spirit, set me free

Every blessing that flows to me

Is a praise song for our destiny

Egbe, sing with me, sing with me

Let this love flow endlessly

From the hidden realms into my days

Let my whole life be your praise

Egbe Orun, I remember you

Egbe Orun, I honor you

Egbe mi, heavenly friends

Walk with me, walk with me

Now and always, walk with me

ORIKI TO EGBE (Praise Poetry)

Oriki Chant written by Chief Oluwole Ifakunle Adetutu Alagbede Manyansa

Egbé *mi Orun, ę bá mi rìn o.*

Egbé *Okun, Egbé llè, e fi omi tú mi!*

Egbé *Abikú, e mo mí ní orúko!*

E ję kí n rìn ní ayé ní ibùkún àti olá!

Walk with me, guide my soul.

Ocean Egbe, Earth Egbe, bathe me in peace.

Spirit children, you knew my name before birth.

Let me walk this life in blessing and honor.

EGBE SUPPORTS ME (Praise Poetry)

*Òrìṣà Song Written by Chief Oluwole Ifakunle Adetutu Alagbede
Manyansa*

My Egbe supports it is true

For your heavenly companions walk faithfully with me in every place.

In the quiet of the morning, falling of the dew, when my spirit starts to rise,
I hear the whispers of my Ẹgbé calling me from the sides

They say, "Child of light, don't fear the storms you face,"

For my heavenly companions walk faithfully with me in every place, sky
to sea, from forest to stone.

My Egbe stand beside me- my true spiritual home.

When I dance, my Egbe dance; when I pray, they rise,

A thousand shining companions circling me in the skies.

In the quiet of the morning, when my spirit starts to rise, I hear the whispers
of my Ẹgbé calling from the sides.

They say, " Child of the light, don't fear the storms, child of light,

don't fear the storms" in a glimmer of a moment my Egbe's support is
in swarms

For my heavenly companions my mirror's shadow walk faithfully with
me in every situation they fill me with glee.

As above so below....

From sky to sea, from forest to stone, My Egbe stand beside me-

my true spiritual home.

When I dance, my Egbe dance;

when I pray, they rise,

A thousand shining companions circling me from the other sides.

CONTEMPORARY PRAYERS

Prayer for Egbe Connection

This is a prayer I developed for those who want to acknowledge and connect with their Egbe without formal initiation. It can be used during personal devotion, meditation, or when making offerings.

I call to my Egbe, my soul group in Orun. You who witnessed my agreements before I descended into Aiye. You who remember what I came here to do when I have forgotten. You who orchestrate my path and open doors in alignment with my destiny.

I acknowledge you today. I remember that we are not separate. I am your earthly expression; you are my heavenly continuity. What exists in Orun exists in Aiye through me.

Guide my steps. Illuminate my path. Bring the right people at the right time. Close doors that lead away from my purpose. Open doors that lead toward my highest expression.

I am grateful for your witness. I am grateful for your orchestration. I am grateful for the agreements we hold together.

Ase. Ase. Ase.

Prayer for Alignment with Soul Agreements

Use this prayer when you feel confused about your direction, when you're facing a major decision, or when you want to reaffirm your commitment to living in alignment with what your Ori chose.

I return to the truth of my agreements. Before I was born, my Ori made choices. My Egbe witnessed those choices. My Enikeji Orun holds the memory of what I came here to do.

Today, I ask for clarity. Show me where I am living in alignment. Show me where I have drifted from my path. Give me the courage to correct what needs correcting.

I am willing to release what no longer serves my soul's purpose. I am willing to embrace what I have been avoiding. I trust the orchestration, even when I cannot see the full picture.

As above, so below. As within, so without. Let my inner knowing match my outer living.

Ase.

Prayer from the Egbe Prayer I Use Daily

This is a version of the prayer I mention in Chapter 1, which I use when I need things to flow, when I'm navigating situations that require support, or simply to start my day in connection.

May everyone I encounter today be a part of my Egbe. May every hand that touches my work be aligned with my highest good. May every door I approach open if it serves my path, and close if it does not. May I recognize my soul family when they appear. May I trust the orchestration, even when it looks like an obstacle.

Egbe, I remember you. Remember me.

Invocation for Ose Egbe (Regular Egbe Observance)

If you choose to establish a regular practice of acknowledging your Egbe (which can be done weekly, monthly, or as you feel called), this invocation can be used when making offerings.

I greet you, my Egbe. I come today with offerings of gratitude. I bring [name your offerings: water, honey, sweets, fruit, etc.] I bring my presence and my remembrance.

I have not forgotten you. Though I walk in Aiye with its forgetting, I remember. You are my soul family. I am your earthly expression.

Accept these offerings as a sign of our continued relationship. Continue to guide my path. Continue to orchestrate my good. Continue to witness my journey and hold space for my becoming.

All that is sweet, may my life be sweet. All that is nourishing, may my path be nourished. All that is given in love, may love return multiplied.

Ase.

APPENDIX B

Common Offerings to Egbe

Offerings to Egbe are not about bribery or transaction. They are about reciprocity, acknowledgment, and maintaining relationship. When you make an offering, you are saying: "I remember you. I honor our connection. I am present in this relationship."

The following list includes traditional offerings used in Isese practice as well as contemporary adaptations. Use what is available and accessible to you. Sincerity matters more than specific items.

Traditional Offerings

Fruits

- Bananas (*ogede*)
- Sugarcane (*ireke*)
- Coconut (*agbon*)
- Oranges
- Any fresh seasonal fruits

Sweets and Treats

- Honey (*oyin*)
- Candy and chocolates
- Cookies and biscuits
- Roasted or boiled groundnuts/peanuts (*epa*)
- Popcorn

Traditional Prepared Foods

- *Ekuru* (white bean cake, no palm oil or pepper)
- *Aadun* (sweetened corn flour with palm oil)
- *Akara* (fried bean cakes)
- *Moin moin* (steamed bean pudding)
- *Eko* (fermented corn pudding)

Other Items

- Cool, clean water
- White kola nut (*obi*)
- Palm oil (*epo pupa*)
- Gin or other clear spirits
- Shea butter (*ori*)

Contemporary/Accessible Offerings

If you don't have access to traditional items, or if you're practicing in a context where these aren't available, you can offer:

- Any sweet treats children would enjoy
- Fresh fruit of any kind

- Honey or sweet syrups
- Cookies, candies, chocolate
- Sweet drinks (fruit juice, sweet tea)
- Toys or small playful items (Egbe appreciates childlike joy)
- Fresh flowers
- Clean water

Guidelines for Making Offerings

Cleanliness matters. Approach your offerings with clean hands and in clean space.

State your intention. Speak to your Egbe when you make offerings. Tell them who you are (your name and your mother's name is traditional), why you're making the offering, and what you're grateful for or asking for.

Placement. If you have an Egbe shrine or pot, offerings can be placed there. If not, offerings can be placed on a clean white cloth in a dedicated space, or taken to nature (riverside, base of a large tree, garden).

Disposal. Offerings that are perishable should be removed after a day or as they begin to spoil. They can be placed in nature or disposed of with respect. Non-perishables like toys can remain as part of your shrine.

Share the offering. Traditionally, after Egbe has received the spiritual essence of the food, the physical food can be shared and eaten by people present. This is not required, but it's beautiful practice.

Frequency. There is no required frequency. Some people do Ose Egbe weekly, some monthly, some only when moved to. Pay attention to your dreams, intuition, and life circumstances for signs that your Egbe is requesting attention.

A Note About Offerings Without Initiation

You do not need to be initiated to Egbe to make simple offerings of acknowledgment. What you cannot do without initiation is conduct formal ceremonies, work with the Awe pot, or lead Egbe rituals for others.

Simple offerings of fruit, water, honey, and sincere prayer are appropriate for anyone who feels called to honor their soul group connection.

APPENDIX C

Journaling Prompts for Soul Group Work

These prompts are designed to help you deepen your understanding of your own Egbe connection, explore your soul agreements, and integrate the concepts from this book.

Prompts for Recognizing Your Egbe

- Who in your life feels like "soul family" rather than just a friend or relative? What makes that connection different from other relationships?
- Describe a time when you met someone and felt instant recognition, as if you'd known them before. What happened in that relationship?
- What patterns have repeated across multiple relationships in your life? What might these patterns be trying to show you about your soul agreements?
- Recall a "coincidence" that felt like more than coincidence. How might this have been orchestrated by your Egbe?
- What doors have closed in your life despite your best efforts to keep them open? Looking back, what did those closings make possible?

Prompts for Understanding Your Soul Agreements

- If you could identify one core lesson you've been learning your entire life, what would it be? How has this lesson shown up in different forms?
- What gifts or abilities have always felt natural to you, as if you came into this life already knowing them? What might this suggest about your soul agreements?
- What do you feel most called to contribute to the world? Where does this calling feel like it comes from?
- Are there any relationships in your life that feel "fated" or unavoidable, even if they're challenging? What might you and this person have agreed to learn together?
- What aspects of your life feel most aligned right now? What aspects feel most out of alignment? What's the difference in how these areas feel in your body?

Prompts for Connecting with Your Enikeji Orun

- If the eternal part of you could send a message to your current human self, what would it say?
- What does your Enikeji Orun (eternal soul self) know that your personality sometimes forgets?
- In moments of deep stillness or meditation, what voice or knowing emerges that feels different from your everyday thoughts?
- What would change in your life if you trusted that part of you is always in Orun, always connected to the larger picture?
- Write a letter to your Enikeji Orun. Ask any questions you have. Then write the response that comes.

Prompts for Living the Law of Correspondence

- "As above, so below." What exists in your inner world that you see reflected in your outer circumstances?
- Where in your life do you see evidence of spiritual agreements manifesting as physical experiences?
- If your current life circumstances are a mirror, what are they reflecting back to you about your beliefs, patterns, or agreements?
- What would shift in your external life if you changed something in your internal world? What internal change feels most important right now?
- How might your Egbe be orchestrating your current circumstances for your highest good, even if it doesn't feel good in the moment?

APPENDIX D

Signs of Strong Egbe Connection

The following signs may indicate that your Egbe connection is particularly active or that your Egbe is calling for your attention. These are not diagnostic criteria, just patterns that have been observed across traditional practice and my own experience with clients.

General Signs of Strong Egbe Connection

- Recurring dreams of groups of people, especially children or peers
- Dreams of being by water with others
- Dreams of gatherings, celebrations, or meetings in unfamiliar but familiar-feeling places
- Feeling like you don't quite belong in the physical world
- Persistent sense of homesickness for a place you can't identify
- Strong intuitive or psychic abilities from childhood
- Tendency to feel "different" from family of origin
- Deep connections with people who feel like soul family
- Life characterized by meaningful coincidences and synchronicities

Signs Egbe May Be Requesting Attention

- Frequent unexplained loss of items
- Chronic relationship difficulties despite sincere effort
- Recurring obstacles in areas that "should" be working
- Persistent dreams of children asking for food, water, or attention
- Dreams of being called somewhere or by someone
- Feeling stuck in life despite trying many solutions
- Sudden increase in intuitive messages or downloads
- Health issues without clear physical cause
- Sense of something being "off" that you can't explain

Signs of Alignment with Egbe

- Life flowing with unusual ease
- Right people appearing at right times
- Opportunities emerging without excessive effort
- Dreams that provide clear guidance
- Sense of being supported by unseen forces
- Creative inspiration flowing freely
- Relationships characterized by recognition and depth
- Feeling of being "on path" even during challenges

What to Do If You Recognize These Signs

If you recognize many of these signs in your life, you might:

- Begin a regular practice of acknowledgment (simple offerings, prayer, meditation)
- Keep a dream journal to track messages from your Egbe

- Seek Ifa divination from a legitimate priest if you want clarity about your specific situation
- Read the chapters on soul agreements and alignment for deeper understanding
- Work with the journaling prompts in Appendix C
- If strongly called, explore whether Egbe initiation is appropriate for your path (this should be done through proper channels with legitimate elders, not through online courses or self-initiation)

APPENDIX E

Resources for Further Study

Books on Egbe

- *Egbe: The Heavenly Mates of Every Human* (2024) by Ayo Salami — The foundational text on Egbe, recently reprinted. Essential reading for anyone serious about understanding this tradition.
- *Egbe Orun: Comrades of Heaven* (2020) by Ifayemisi Elebuibon — Beautiful exploration of Egbe from within the Elebuibon lineage in Osogbo.
- *Egbe Orun: Path to Self Discovery* (2023) by Ifayemisi Elebuibon — Continues Elebuibon's work on Egbe with practical applications.
- *Egbe: The Sacred Tie That Binds* (2016) by Baale Olukunmi Omikemi Egbelade — Another valuable perspective on Egbe practice.

Books on Yoruba Cosmology and Ifa

- *Sixteen Mythological Stories of Ifa* by Wande Abimbola — Classic introduction to Ifa mythology.
- *Ifa: An Exposition of the Ifa Literary Corpus* by Wande Abimbola — Scholarly foundation for understanding Ifa.

- *Ifa Divination: Communication Between Gods and Men in West Africa* by William Bascom — Academic but accessible overview of Ifa divination.
- *The Handbook of Yoruba Religious Concepts* by Baba Ifa Karade — Good introductory overview for those new to Yoruba cosmology.

Books on Akashic Records and Soul Work

- *Accessing the Akashic Records: A Practical Guide to Healing, Clarity, and Empowerment (2024)* by Dr. La Toya Davis — My comprehensive guide to Akashic Records work.

Books on Soul Contracts and Pre-Birth Planning

- *Your Soul's Plan* by Robert Schwartz — A pre-birth planning model that many readers find helpful for contextualizing soul agreements.
- *Journey of Souls* by Michael Newton — A popular framework for between-life narratives and soul choices.
- *Sacred Contracts* by Caroline Myss — Helpful language for archetypes and life lessons as agreements.

Books on Universal Laws and Metaphysics

- *The Kybalion* by Three Initiates
- *The Seven Spiritual Laws of Success* by Deepak Chopra

Finding Legitimate Practitioners

If you're seeking Ifa divination or considering Egbe initiation, it's important to work with legitimate practitioners rooted in tradition. Some guidance:

- Ask about their lineage and training
- Be wary of anyone who learned primarily from books or online courses
- Seek referrals from people you trust
- Be cautious of exorbitant fees or fear-based messaging
- Trust your intuition about whether someone is aligned

APPENDIX F

Pronunciation Key

Yoruba pronunciation follows these general patterns:

Vowels are pronounced as in Spanish or Italian (pure vowels):

"A" as in "father"
"E" as in "bed"
"I" as in "see"
"O" as in "go"
"U" as in "food"

"GB" is pronounced as a single sound (lips come together for both letters simultaneously)

Accent marks indicate tone (high, mid, low) which affects meaning

Double vowels are pronounced longer, not repeated

Note: This glossary represents the terminology as used in this book. Yoruba terms may have variant spellings and pronunciations across different lineages and regions. Metaphysical terms may carry different nuances in different spiritual traditions. Definitions here are intended to support your understanding of the specific framework presented in these pages.

APPENDIX G

Glossary of Yoruba, Diasporic and Metaphysical Terms

This glossary includes Yoruba terms from Isese tradition and metaphysical/universal terms used throughout this book. It also includes related terms you may encounter in further study of Egbe, Yoruba cosmology, and soul group concepts. All definitions reflect usage within this book's framework and may vary across lineages, regions, and practitioners. The bridge between Yoruba cosmology and universal metaphysics is central to this work, so you'll find both traditional and contemporary terminology defined here.

YORUBA & DIASPORIC TERMS

Abiku (ah-BEE-koo): Literally "born to die." Refers to children who die young and repeatedly return through the same parents in a cycle of birth and death. Associated with specific Egbe classes, particularly Paaka Inu Abiku/Olugbogero. Traditional practice includes ritual markings and ceremonies to anchor the child to earthly life.

Afowofa (ah-foh-WOH-fah): Self-created circumstances; the situations and conditions we generate through our own choices. Represents the role of free will within the destiny framework.

Aiye (ah-YEE-yeh): The physical world; earth; the realm of incarnation where souls experience human life. The counterpart to Orun (the spiritual realm). In this book, Aiye represents the "below" in "as above, so below."

Ajala (ah-JAH-lah): The celestial potter in Orun who manufactures Ori (spiritual heads). According to Yoruba cosmology, each soul must choose an Ori from Ajala's workshop before incarnating. Ajala's work varies in quality, which accounts for differences in destiny outcomes.

Akunlegba (ah-KOON-leh-bah): Literally "that which is received kneeling." The divine logistics system; the spiritual mechanism that orchestrates circumstances to fulfill soul agreements. Includes the family, place, and conditions into which one is born.

Akunleyan (ah-koon-LEH-yahn): Literally "that which is chosen kneeling." The destiny selected by kneeling before Olodumare before birth; the choices made by the soul about what this lifetime will include.

Ase (ah-SHAY): Divine power; the force of creation and transformation; the authority to make things happen. Often used as an affirmation meaning "so be it" or "may it be so."

Awe (ah-WEH): The consecrated pot that serves as the primary symbol and connection point for Egbe. Received during Egbe initiation and used for ongoing communication and offerings.

Ayanmo (ah-YAHN-moh): The fixed, unchangeable aspects of destiny; that which is sealed at incarnation. Includes elements like family of birth, biological sex, and certain karmic patterns that cannot be altered but can be responded to with agency.

Babalawo (bah-bah-LAH-woh): A priest of Ifa; one who practices Ifa divination. Literally "father of secrets" or "father of the mysteries." The masculine equivalent of Iyanifa.

Candomble (kahn-dohm-BLEH): An Afro-Brazilian religion derived from Yoruba traditions, preserving many Orisa (called Orixas) and cosmological concepts that survived the Trans-Atlantic slave trade.

Ebo (EH-boh): Offering or sacrifice made to spiritual forces; the ritual act of giving to maintain reciprocal relationships with Orisa, Egbe, ancestors, or other spiritual entities.

Efun (eh-FOON): White chalk used in ritual practice; represents purity, coolness, and spiritual clarity.

Egbe (EHG-beh): Literally "group" or "society." Your spiritual collective; the soul group you belong to across lifetimes. The foundation concept of this book.

Egbe Orun (EHG-beh oh-ROON): "Heavenly society" or "heavenly group." Your soul group in the spiritual realm; the collective consciousness that holds your pre-birth agreements and supports your journey in Aiye.

Egun (eh-GOON): Ancestors; the spirits of the deceased who maintain connection with and influence over the living. Distinguished from Egbe (soul group companions) and Orisa (divine forces).

Ekuru (eh-KOO-roo): A traditional food made from ground beans, steamed without oil or pepper. Commonly used as an offering to Egbe.

Emi (eh-MEE): Life force; the breath of life given by Olodumare to animate the soul. The vital energy that enlivens the physical body.

Enikeji Orun/Inikeji Orun (eh-nee-KEH-jee oh-ROON): Your "heavenly double" or "heavenly counterpart"; the eternal, individuated aspect of your being that exists in Orun while you inhabit Aiye. Your eternal soul self that carries essence across lifetimes. Also spelled Elekeji or Eni keji Orun.

Epe (EH-peh): Curse; a form of spiritual harm that can affect one's destiny unfolding.

Ese (eh-SHEH): Feet or legs; in destiny context, represents hard work and personal effort required to actualize one's chosen path.

Espiritismo (es-pee-ree-TEEZ-moh): A spiritual practice that developed in the Caribbean, particularly Cuba and Puerto Rico, involving communication with spirits and ancestors through mediumship. Influences many diaspora practitioners' understanding of spiritual work.

Esu (EH-shoo): The Orisa of the crossroads, communication, and divine messenger. Facilitates connection between realms and delivers offerings to other Orisa. Often misunderstood as "trickster" but more accurately understood as the force that ensures accountability and communication.

Ibeji (ee-BEH-jee): The sacred twins; Orisa associated with duality, children, and doubling. In the diaspora, Egbe concepts were sometimes syncretized with or interpreted through Ibeji worship.

Idigba Egbe/Igba Didi (ee-DEEG-bah EHG-beh): Ritual performed to separate a person from harmful Egbe agreements or transform problematic covenants into beneficial ones. Used particularly when agreements interfere with marriage, childbearing, or cause premature death patterns.

Ifa (ee-FAH): The divination system and body of wisdom associated with the Orisa Orunmila; the sacred practice used to access information about destiny and alignment. Contains 256 Odu (sacred verses) that hold the wisdom of existence.

Ikoko Egbe (ee-KOH-koh EHG-beh): The Egbe pot; the ritual container used for communication and offerings to Egbe.

Ile Ori (ee-LEH oh-REE): "House of the Head"; a physical shrine containing the Ibori (symbolic representation of inner head) used for Ori worship.

Ipin (ee-PEEN): Portion; the share of destiny assigned by divine forces.

Irari Egbe (ee-RAH-ree EHG-beh): Egbe initiation; the ritual process by which one formally reconnects with and strengthens the relationship with their Egbe.

Irunmole (ee-roon-MOH-leh): Primordial consciousness; the earliest expressions of divine intelligence present at creation, before the Orisa were specified. The 401 original divine forces.

Isese (ee-SHEH-sheh): "Tradition" or "origin"; the traditional religion and spiritual practice of the Yoruba people. The ancestral path from which Yoruba spiritual concepts emerge.

Iwa-pele (ee-WAH peh-LEH): Good or balanced character; the quality of living in alignment that produces ease and good fortune. Essential for actualizing one's destiny potential.

Iyanifa (ee-yah-NEE-fah): A female priest of Ifa; a woman who practices Ifa divination. The feminine equivalent of Babalawo.

Kadara (kah-DAH-rah): Predetermined destiny; another term for the life path chosen before birth.

Kola Nut (Obi) : Sacred nuts used in divination and offerings throughout Yoruba tradition. Four-lobed kola nuts (obi oloju merin) are particularly significant in ritual practice.

Lucumi (loo-koo-MEE): Also known as Santeria or Regla de Ocha; the Cuban Orisa tradition that preserved Yoruba religious practices through the period of enslavement. A major diaspora tradition.

Misa (MEE-sah): A spiritual gathering, particularly in Espiritismo and related traditions, where ancestors and spirits are invoked to deliver messages and provide guidance.

Obatala (oh-bah-TAH-lah): The Orisa of creation, purity, and consciousness; the divine sculptor who molds physical forms (including Ori) from clay. Associated with whiteness, clarity, and the heights of creation.

Obi (oh-BEE): Kola nut; used in divination (obi dida) and as offerings throughout Yoruba practice.

Odu (oh-DOO): The sacred verses of Ifa; the 256 configurations that contain all human wisdom and experience. Each Odu contains stories, prescriptions, and guidance.

Oko Orun/Aya Orun (OH-koh oh-ROON / AH-yah oh-ROON): Spiritual spouse; a heavenly husband (Oko) or wife (Aya) relationship that can interfere with earthly partnerships when unacknowledged or unaddressed.

Olodumare (oh-loh-doo-MAH-reh): The Supreme Being; Source; the infinite consciousness from which all existence emerges. Also called Olorun or Eledumare.

Omi Igbagbe (oh-MEE eeg-BAHG-beh): The "river of forgetfulness"; the veil that causes souls to forget their pre-birth agreements upon incarnation.

Opele (oh-PEH-leh): The divination chain used by Babalawo/Iyanifa in Ifa divination; consists of eight half-seed pods connected by chain.

Ori (oh-REE): Literally "head." Your inner consciousness, destiny, and personal deity. Ori Inu (inner head) is the spiritual aspect that holds your destiny blueprint and represents your connection to divine consciousness. Ori Ode (outer head) is the physical head.

Ori Ibi (oh-REE ee-BEE): A "bad" or "confused head"; a state of misalignment with one's destiny.

Ori Ire (oh-REE ee-REH): A "good" or "wise head"; a state of alignment with one's destiny.

Orisa (oh-REE-shah): Divine energies; universal forces that govern aspects of nature and consciousness. Includes Obatala, Ogun, Oshun, Yemoja, Shango, and many others. (Also spelled Orisha in some traditions.)

Orun (oh-ROON): The spiritual realm; heaven; the dimension of existence where souls originate, where Egbe resides, and where souls return after physical death. The counterpart to Aiye (earth). In this book, Orun represents the "above" in "as above, so below."

Orunmila (oh-roon-MEE-lah): The Orisa of wisdom, divination, and destiny; the witness to all Ori selections; the keeper of Ifa wisdom. Present when every soul chose its path.

Ose Egbe (oh-SHEH EHG-beh): Regular observance to honor and connect with Egbe; typically includes offerings of water, sweets, fruits, and prayers. Can be done weekly or at intervals that feel appropriate.

Osun/Oshun (oh-SHOON): The Orisa of fresh water, love, fertility, and abundance. Associated with sweetness, beauty, and the flow of blessings.

Palo Mayombe (PAH-loh mah-YOHM-beh): An Afro-Cuban religion with roots in Central African (primarily Kongolese) spiritual traditions. Works extensively with ancestor spirits and natural forces.

Taboo (Eewo) : Prohibitions or restrictions revealed through divination that an individual must observe to maintain spiritual balance and protection.

METAPHYSICAL & UNIVERSAL TERMS

Akash/Akasha (ah-KAHSH): Sanskrit term meaning "ether," "air," or "space." The fundamental essence underlying all things in the material world; energy in its earliest state before manifestation. The root of "Akashic."

Akashic Records: An energetic field or vibrational body of consciousness containing every thought, choice, experience, and possibility from every soul across all lifetimes. Not a physical library but an infinite field of soul-level information accessible through specific practices.

Alignment: The state of living in accordance with one's soul agreements, destiny, and authentic self. Characterized by flow, synchronicity, and a sense of rightness. The opposite of resistance or misalignment.

As Above, So Below: The foundational principle of the Law of Correspondence from Hermetic philosophy. Indicates that what exists in spiritual realms mirrors physical realms, and what exists within consciousness manifests in external circumstances.

Claircognizance: Clear knowing; the intuitive ability to receive information through direct knowing without logical explanation. One of several "clair" senses (alongside clairvoyance, clairaudience, clairsentience).

Collective Consciousness: The shared awareness or knowing that exists among groups of souls or humanity as a whole. Egbe represents one form of collective consciousness.

Correspondence: See "Law of Correspondence."

Destiny: The path chosen by the soul before incarnation; the experiences, lessons, relationships, and purposes one agreed to in pre-birth planning. In Yoruba terms, encompasses Ayanmo, Akunleyan, and Akunlegba.

Downloads: Intuitive or spiritual information received suddenly and completely, often experienced as knowing that arrives fully formed rather than through step-by-step reasoning.

Eternal Soul Self: The aspect of consciousness that exists beyond physical incarnation; the "you" that was before birth and continues after death. In Yoruba cosmology, this is your Enikeji Orun.

Flow State: The experience of moving through life with ease and alignment; when actions feel effortless and circumstances arrange themselves supportively. Indicates harmony with soul agreements.

Fractal: A pattern that repeats at every scale; used in this book to describe how the individual soul reflects the soul group, which reflects universal consciousness. You are a fractal of the infinite.

Free Will: The capacity to make choices within the framework of destiny; the ability to respond to circumstances even when those circumstances were pre-agreed. Works in concert with, not against, soul agreements.

Hermetic Philosophy: Ancient spiritual philosophy attributed to Hermes Trismegistus, containing principles including Mentalism, Correspondence, Vibration, Polarity, Rhythm, Cause and Effect, and Gender. Source of "as above, so below."

Higher Self: In metaphysical terminology, the aspect of self that exists beyond ego and physical limitation; often used interchangeably with soul self or Enikeji Orun, though subtle distinctions exist across traditions.

Incarnation: The process of a soul taking physical form; being born into a body; entering Aiye from Orun.

Infinite Field: Universal consciousness; the ground of all being; the dimension where all souls, all information, and all possibilities exist simultaneously. Called by many names across traditions: Orun, the Akash, Source, the Unified Field, Universal Mind.

Karma: The principle that actions generate corresponding consequences; energy that returns in kind. Related to but distinct from Yoruba concepts of destiny and character.

Law of Cause and Effect: Hermetic principle stating that every cause has an effect and every effect has a cause; nothing happens by chance.

Law of Correspondence: The Hermetic principle that patterns repeat across all levels of existence: as above, so below; as within, so without; as the universe, so the soul. Central to this book's framework.

Law of Oneness: The principle that everything is connected; all is one; separation is illusion. All souls emerge from and return to the same Source.

Masters, Teachers, and Loved Ones (MTLOs): In Akashic Records terminology, the spiritual presences encountered when accessing the Records who provide guidance and information.

Microcosm/Macrocosm: The principle that the small reflects the large; the individual contains the pattern of the universe; your soul journey mirrors cosmic evolution.

Multidimensional: Existing across multiple planes or realms simultaneously; the understanding that you are present in both Aiye and Orun at once.

Orchestration: The coordinated arrangement of circumstances by spiritual forces (particularly Egbe) to support soul agreements; how synchronicities are created and doors open or close.

Past Life: A previous incarnation; an earthly life lived before the current one. Your Enikeji Orun carries patterns, lessons, and unfinished work from past lives.

Pre-Birth Agreements: Choices made by the soul before incarnation regarding what experiences, relationships, lessons, and purposes this lifetime will contain. Witnessed by Egbe in Orun.

Reincarnation: The cycle of souls returning to physical form across multiple lifetimes; the soul's journey through successive incarnations.

Resonance: The felt sense of alignment or recognition; the experience of something being "right" or familiar at a soul level. Used to identify soul family, true path, and aligned choices.

Soul Agreements: See "Pre-Birth Agreements."

Soul Cluster/Soul Group: In metaphysical terminology, a collective of souls who incarnate together across lifetimes to support mutual growth. The universal equivalent of Egbe.

Soul Contract: An agreement made between souls before incarnation; can include relationships, lessons, or purposes to be fulfilled together. Archived in the Akashic Records and held by Egbe.

Soul Family: Those souls with whom you share deep connection across lifetimes; members of your soul group who incarnate together repeatedly. In Yoruba terms, your Egbe who have also taken human form.

Source: Universal consciousness; God; the infinite; the origin and destination of all souls. In Yoruba cosmology, Olodumare.

Sovereignty: Self-governance; the principle that you are the ultimate authority in your spiritual life. Spiritual sovereignty means working WITH spiritual forces rather than being dependent on or controlled by them.

Synchronicity: Meaningful coincidence; events that align in ways that seem beyond chance, often orchestrated by Egbe or spiritual forces to communicate guidance or confirmation.

Universal Consciousness: The infinite field of awareness from which all individual consciousness emerges; the "All" that contains every soul, every possibility, every dimension. Called Orun, Source, God, the Akash, the Unified Field across traditions.

Veil: The forgetting that occurs at birth; the separation between conscious awareness and soul-level knowing. Called Omi Igbagbe (river of forgetfulness) in Yoruba cosmology.

Vibration/Frequency: The energetic signature or quality of consciousness; all things vibrate at particular frequencies. Alignment involves matching your vibration to your soul's truth.

Acknowledgments

This book was not an easy task, and I want to take a moment to acknowledge some very special energies that contributed to the fulfillment of this project.

There is not a day that goes by that I am not eternally grateful for my babies (who are teens now). They are my biggest cheerleaders and the walking epitome of "you can do this." Everything I do, I do to show you what's possible when you live according to your soul's truth rather than the world's expectations. May you always know your Egbe is with you.

My parents, who are watching and supporting me from Orun.

Araba Chief Ifayemi Elebuibon and Iyalorisa Oyelola Ajibola Elebuibon: Thank you for welcoming me into your home and into this tradition. The initiation you facilitated changed the course of my life.

My godfather in Ifa, Chief Oluwole Ifakunle Adetutu Alagbede Manyansa (aka The Babalawo of Harlem): Thank you for listening when Spirit said Egbe, even though it meant sending me somewhere you couldn't follow. Your willingness to honor what was right over what was convenient has been the hallmark of our relationship, and I appreciate that you teach me without limits.

Funlayo Wood, Ph.D., and Ase Ire, Inc.: Thank you for being the familiar face when I landed in Nigeria, not knowing what awaited me. I see the work that you do for our community, and you inspire me consistently.

Oba "Ifasina" Tsare, Corine "Osunbgemi" Stancil, Jalisa "Bamike" Boynes, and Iya Efunlayo Maxey: Thank you for reading my early versions of this work and convincing me that I wasn't crazy. Your encouragement did not go unnoticed, and it definitely contributed to the final version of this book.

Every client who has trusted me with their Records, their questions, and their healing: your courage to show up and do the work reminds me daily why I do this.

And to my Egbe in Orun: Thank you for never giving up on me, even when I wasn't listening. Thank you for the orchestration that led to this book. Thank you for remembering who I am when I forgot.

Mo dupe. I am grateful.

Muso! Muso! Musooo!

About the Author

Dr. La Toya Davis (Ìyá Ẹgbẹ́níkẹ́) is an oracle, spiritual teacher, Egbe priestess (Ẹlẹ́gbẹ́), Yayi Nkisi Malongo, and the founder of CHI Healing Institute. With decades of experience across African Traditional Religions and diasporic lineages, including Ìṣẹ̀ṣe, Lucumí, and Palo Mayombe, she teaches spiritual sovereignty, personal responsibility, and ancestral intelligence, supporting people in major life transitions to clarify who they are becoming and what their soul is calling forward now.

Initiated into Egbe in Osogbo, Nigeria in 2015 under Iyalorisa Oyelola Elebuibon, Dr. La Toya brings a rare blend of traditional devotion and modern application to her teachings. Her practice is further informed by the Akashic Records, where she supports clients and students in exploring soul agreements, life themes, and the deeper patterns that shape identity, relationships, and purpose.

She is the author of *Accessing the Akashic Records: A Practical Guide to Healing, Clarity, and Empowerment*, *The Akashic Record Journal*, and the *Path to the Ancestors* book series. She also developed the SHIFT Protocol™, a transformation framework that guides individuals from insight to embodiment through aligned, soul-rooted action.

Dr. La Toya teaches globally through CHI Healing Institute as an international speaker, facilitator, and retreat guide, leading immersive experiences and trainings that help seekers move from spiritual insight into embodied, soul-aligned living. She also hosts the Soul Aligned Living YouTube show, where she shares teachings on spiritual sovereignty, soul agreements, and ancestral intelligence.

Connect with Dr. La Toya Davis

Website: www.chihealinginstitute.com
www.drlatoyadavis.com

YouTube: Soul Aligned Living @dr.latoyadavis

Instagram and Facebook: @chihealinginstitute

Books By Dr. La Toya Davis

Egbe and Soul Agreements

- *Egbe Orun: The Soul Group That Remembers You*
  Understand your pre-birth agreements and the unseen
  relationships shaping your life, so you can live with greater
  clarity, alignment, and self-trust.

The Akashic Records

- *Accessing the Akashic Records: A Practical Guide to Healing,
  Clarity, and Empowerment*
  Learn how to access the Records in a grounded way, so
  you can receive clear guidance, heal patterns, and make
  aligned decisions.
- *The Akashic Record Journal: A Guided Journal to Support Accessing
  and Exploring Your Akashic Records*
  A guided companion to help you strengthen your practice, track
  what you receive, and deepen trust in your spiritual discernment.

Path to the Ancestors

- *Path to the Ancestors: 33 Prayers, Prompts, and Rituals for Healing and Connection*
  A 33-day devotional journey to honor your lineage, deepen connection, and move through healing with consistent spiritual practice.
- *Path to the Ancestors: 33 Day Guided Journal for Healing, Connection, and Personal Growth*
  Daily prompts and reflection space to support release, integration, and transformation, so your ancestral work becomes lived experience.

Interactive Learning and Guided Practice

- *Odu Ifá: A Coloring and Activity Book to Learn the 16 Major Odu*
  An interactive introduction to the 16 Major Odu, designed to make learning approachable, memorable, and engaging.
- *Gratitude Journal: 6 Week Journey to Creating an Attitude of Gratitude*
  A six-week practice that trains your focus, shifts your perspective, and anchors gratitude as a daily way of being.

To explore readings, classes, and certification programs,
visit chihealinginstitute.com.